DIRTY KNEES
and
GREEN THUMBS

a guide to planting the extraordinary and seeing the impossible grow.

BRYAN MEADOWS

BRYAN MEADOWS MINISTRIES
P.O. Box 161221
Atlanta, Georgia 30321

ISBN: 148391948X
ISBN-13: 978-1483919485

All artwork done by CJ Hudgins and Design Cortex
www.designcortex.net

All scripture quotations, unless otherwise indicated, are taken from the King James Version (Authorized Version). First published in 1611.

Table of Contents

DEDICATION

I dedicate this book to the ultimate planter, my wife, Patrice Meadows. You took a chance on me. Through faith, you saw me beyond where I was, and believed that I was destined for more. You sowed into me for years and didn't see a harvest, but you believed. Thank you. And to my daughter, Amirah Lee, you are my inspiration. Every day you challenge me to be patient, loving, kind, and gentle. You grow me. And to my mother, Janet Harris, you have always been there for me. You have been a great example. You are my personal intercessor, and my greatest cheerleader. I love you mom. I dedicate this book to my ladies.

Bryan Meadows

PREFACE

So this is a book about planting churches? I guess we can say that, but to be quite honest, I think it is about more than just church planting. If I could define this book, I would call it a challenge. I remember one day I was watching a basketball game. Apparently the star player of the team was not playing up to par. The coach, very upset with him, called a time out and as the player approached the bench the coach pushed him violently. The player became irate and started yelling at the coach. The player's team members grabbed him and pushed him against the wall, "GET YOUR HEAD IN THE GAME," they yelled. Eventually this player, and the coach, calmed down and got focused. The star player went back into the game, scored four straight three pointers to clutch the win for the team. That is what I want this book to be for you. The same way that star player needed just a little push for his potential to be realized and his gift to be stretched, that is what I endeavor for this book to be for you. That is what I want this book to be for a Generation of church planters that are buried in cities. They are unknown. They have no face, no name, no money, but they have a promise. I want this book to become the catalyst for a Generation of water walkers who have been promised that revival is coming to their city, and every day their head is burrowed between their knees, and like Elijah they whisper, "Go look again." This book is not meant to be a "how to" church planting manual, but a church planting challenge.

At the heart of every leader is a vision. Every vision produces expectation, and if you are anything like me, we have BIG expectations. Hey look, if your expectations aren't big enough to make you doubt, most likely they aren't God given. God will always give us a vision that makes us think twice. Expectations are meant to produce a burden. Passion is a coin with two sides. One side of passion is burden, which is the side of responsibility. The other side of passion is grace, which is the side of intimacy and creativity. It is like any relationship. You have the things you "love to do," and the things you "have to do." The things you "love to do" make you want to stay up all night, but it's the things you "have to do" that keep you up all night. It is only when the burden and the grace come together in holy matrimony that passion becomes productive. This book will outline the wedding vows.

The reason I wrote this book is not because I am an expert, but because I am not. Yes, you heard me right. Many times we read "how to" books just to be disappointed that it didn't work for us. We find ourselves depressed and frustrated that the principles that others claimed worked so wonderfully for them caused us to fall on our face. I decided to write this book to challenge the "cookie cutter" model of planting churches. Every fruit begins with a seed and dirt, but the dirt, location, and temperature are all relative. Church Planting is no different. There are some universal rules that we can observe and wisdom we can glean from our predecessors, but what happens when you are called to do something that has never been done before. What happens when no conference can explain it or coach can train it? Now should you commit to being informed and edified by attending great church conference? Yes, please don't misunderstand me, but the purpose of this book is not just to inform but also to activate. The purpose of this book is not to just instruct, but to awaken. This is a guide on how to plant the extraordinary and see the impossible grow.

In a society that prides itself on order and cleanliness, in a world that revels in the glamorous pictures portrayed by facades and images, we rarely get a chance to share in the experiences that grow true leaders. Church Planting is very similar. We love to share the highlights and the videos of us doing great things. But would it not be equally or even more effective to photograph the failures, the staff cancellations, the empty chairs and the bombed messages? Would it not be cool to see a great worship leader singing his or her heart out to crowd of five people? We glory in the end product but forget the power is in the process.

My grandparents owned a farm. When I was young, I can remember traveling to a little small town named Camak, Georgia. The houses in this town were miles apart. Everyone knew each other or was family in some way. As a kid from the city I absolutely hated going down there. My aunts always wanted me to go outside. "GET DIRTY" they would scream. All I wanted to do was watch television. There was something about their generation that understood the value of hard work. Church

Planting is hard work. It takes hours of prayer and labor. If you aren't willing to get your knees dirty and run the risk of failing, you are going to hate this book. Planting requires humility. Planting requires one to be teachable. We need a Generation that isn't afraid to get dirty. Thrust their hands into the soil of their city and toil until revival is grown before their very eyes. You know what they call successful planters? They call people who have found great success at growing things "green thumbs." Why? At some point in your building, planting, growing, your hands become so stained with the color and scent of your passion. Hard work must become natural for a Generation that idolizes the successes of men. We need to know that every successful person has failed, and every person that has failed still has the potential to do great things. This is the reason for this book. For you that are doing great, this book is meant to stretch your potential. For those who are not doing so great, this book is meant to stretch your skill and faith. For those who have yet to start, this book is meant to stretch your expectations and push you out of the boat. Are you ready? Let's begin.

INTRODUCTION

The world that we are living in is definitely complex. The planet used to be a much simpler place. In the past, what was right and wrong was clearly defined and even more clearly fought for. We live in complex times. Cultures are merging, religions are fusing, and the lines of morality are being blurred. Genders are mixing, boundaries are erasing, and the church must now begin to ask the question, "What are we going to do about it?" I believe with my whole heart that the Church is the solution to the world's problems. But how do we engage culture to the degree that our influence is undeniable and we emerge as a culture shaping force that transforms our cities and regions? This is the question that started me on this journey. This is the question that continues to keep me up at night, and if you are reading this book, this is the question that haunts you as well. How do we change the world?

We understand that the world must be reached. This is the Great Commission given to us by our Chief Commander, our Lord and Savior, Jesus Christ.

> And Jesus came and spake unto them, saying, All power is given unto me in heaven and in earth. Go ye therefore, and teach all nations, baptizing them in the name of the Father, and of the Son, and of the Holy Ghost: Teaching them to observe all things whatsoever I have commanded you: and, lo, I am with you always, even unto the end of the world. Amen. (Matthew 28:18-20)

We are to fill the world with the gospel, which is the good news. The good news is that God became a man, gave His life to reconnect us with Him, His identity, His purpose, and His power. The good news is that Jesus died for all, and that the way of salvation has been made. The good news is that with a contrite heart and a broken spirit we approach Jesus with full assurance of faith that He is who He said He is, and that He can do what He said He could do. This is the gospel of Jesus Christ. We are to fill, or make full the world with this message.

God gave this same command to Adam in the book of Genesis.

> And God blessed them, and God said unto them,
> Be fruitful, and multiply, and replenish the earth,
> and subdue it: and have dominion over the fish of
> the sea, and over the fowl of the air, and over
> every living thing that moveth upon the earth.
> (Genesis 1:28)

God gave Adam the command to replenish. The word "replenish" literally means to "fill again." Adam's job was to refill. The world was robbed, it was bankrupt of purpose and power, and Adam's job was to refill it. How was Adam going to do this? One of the things I love about God is that God is a Master Teacher. God never misses the opportunity to enlighten us through life's moments. After God made Adam, he puts Adam to work. Watch this.

> And the LORD God planted a garden eastward
> in Eden; and there he put the man whom he had
> formed. (Gen. 2:8)

> And the LORD God took the man, and put him
> into the garden of Eden to dress it and to keep it.
> (Genesis 2:15)

Do you see that? After God formed Adam, God planted! Wow, what a statement. GOD PLANTED. Now, Jesus teaches us what I call the Principle of Sonship. The Principle of Sonship is the law that governs the behavior and trajectory of a son. Let's look at what Jesus said.

> Then answered Jesus and said unto them,
> Verily, verily, I say unto you, The Son can do
> nothing of himself, but what he seeth the Father
> do: for what things soever he doeth, these also
> doeth the Son likewise. (John 5:19)

The Principle of Sonship says that the son can only do what He sees the Father do. This is a powerful principle. God is going to show Adam how to refill the Earth with purpose and power. He is going to teach Adam to be a Gardener. God is going to show Adam how to plant. Planting was the answer to filling the Earth with God's power and purpose. What was Adam going to plant? Adam's job was to grow the fruit of dominion. We see the formula in Genesis 1:28,

> *And God blessed them, and God said unto them,*
> *Be fruitful, and multiply, and replenish the earth,*
> *and subdue it: and have dominion over the fish*
> *of the sea, and over the fowl of the air, and over*
> *every living thing that moveth upon the earth.*
> *(Genesis 1:28)*

The first thing that God said to Adam is "Be Fruitful." Well how is fruit produced? All fruit begins with a seed. Every seed must be planted. Jesus said,

> *Verily, verily, I say unto you, Except a corn of*
> *wheat fall into the ground and die, it abideth*
> *alone: but if it die, it bringeth forth much fruit.*
> *(John 12:24)*

Adam had to take the seed of dominion and plant it. He had to grow it and cultivate it until that fruit filled the Earth. God's answer for the world is planting. The power of planting was initiated by God. We don't just see this in Genesis. After Adam fell, God continued to plant. We understand that the seed that Jesus is speaking of in John 12:24 is Himself. Jesus was the seed that God planted to redeem the world and refill, or replenish it with His love, purpose and power. Planting is a divine technology that God initiates for the purpose of restoration. This was not just true then, it is also true now. Planting churches is still God's way of growing His dominion in every city and region of the Earth. Dr. C. Peter Wagner says, "The single most effective evangelistic methodology under heaven is planting new churches."

In this book I attempt to scratch the surface of the importance of planting churches. This book will begin speaking on the importance of cities, the burden of church planters, and the dynamics of revival in the 21st century. We will spend time discussing the necessity of strong teams, developing vision, and establishing culture during the planting of kingdom centers. Then we will end by speaking to the need for prayer, patience, and paternal presence to keep us grounded, focused, and accountable. I wanted to make this book as practical as possible, but I did not want to forgo the opportunity to make available valuable statistics and concepts. I have read many church planting and church growth books, and many do not address the spiritual needs to grow a powerful church. We hear a lot about how to grow a church, but there is a difference between a "big" church and a healthy church. Sick churches do not change our communities. If anything, sick churches, hinder the Kingdom of God from advancing by producing stigmatized communities which are against the church and what it seems to represent. This book will speak to the heart of that. I endeavor to address the positives and negatives of the "seeker sensitive" model of church development. Through our journey, my prayer is that, a pattern would emerge, that would become a template for you to do the impossible. Welcome to a planting revolution.

Empty Bellies
and
Soaked Pillows

Chapter One

The Transforming Power of a Burden

I'm Hungry

Have you ever been hungry? I don't mean a hunger that you can ignore. Many times when we say we are hungry, we just mean, "I could eat." But there is a different level of hunger that food cannot satisfy. There is a level of hunger that only a privileged few have an opportunity to feel. The burden of empty bellies is a unique pain to experience. When your stomach is crying out for food it can keep you up at night, it can also wake you up out of your sleep. Have you ever woken up hungry? Have you ever woke up with an insatiable thirst or hunger just to find yourself turning the kitchen upside down? Every woman who has had a baby knows the power of an appetite. Every dreamer, visionary, leader, and entrepreneur has had the honor of hunger. By this time you understand that I am not speaking about natural hunger. The hunger that I am speaking about is the hunger for the impossible. The hunger I am referring to is the hunger to break limits and statistics, to shatter records and shut the mouths of doubters. Anyone called to do anything great has had this hunger. This hunger keeps us pushing on the boundaries and borders of normalcy until we are finally filled.

In the Gospel of John, chapter 4, we see this hunger first hand. After much ministry in Judea, Jesus is prompted to go to Galilee, but something is different. The Bible says in John 4:4,

And he must needs go through Samaria. (John 4:4)

The Young's Literal Translation of the Bible says that it was "behooving him to go through Samaria." The word "behoove," means that it was proper, advantageous, or necessary for Him to take this path. As soon as they get there, Jesus finds himself a seat on Jacob's Well, and the disciples go to the next town to buy food. Now we know the story of the Samaritan woman and how her life was changed by this encounter with Jesus. I love this story. The Samaritan woman comes to a well of "dead water," which is a term used for water that does not move, and she ends up with "living water." Her encounter with Jesus is so massively transformative, that the Bible says that she leaves her water pots.

> *28 The woman then left her water pot, and went her way into the city, and saith to the men, 29 Come, see a man, which told me all things that ever I did: is not this the Christ? 30 Then they went out of the city, and came unto him. (John 4:28-30)*

She comes to the well looking for one thing, but finds something so much more. What she encounters is so great that she leaves every method of human technology behind. She leaves all semblance of her past and begins to tell people about the man she met. In the meantime, the disciples return with food. They ask Jesus to eat, but Jesus is not hungry. They are confused. They have been with Jesus all day. They have not eaten, and they know that the Master has not eaten as well. Something is not right with this picture.

> *31 In the mean while his disciples prayed him, saying, Master, eat. 32 But he said unto them, I have meat to eat that ye know not of. 33 Therefore said the disciples one to another, Hath any man brought him ought to eat? 34 Jesus saith unto them, My meat is to do the will of him that sent me, and to finish his work.*
> *(John 4:31-34)*

This story is loaded with prophetic significance. I think it is interesting that his disciples "prayed him" saying "Master, eat." The word "prayed" literally means to beseech, to entreat, earnest request, or to beg. They were pleading with Jesus, "Please eat something." There are moments in our lives where the people closest to us won't understand that we have had an intense appetite shift. An appetite shift is when what you desire changes. This happens in the life of the sinner when they no longer find fulfillment in a life of sin. The sinner begins to seek more. Seeking is always marked by questions. After a sinner finds Christ, they no longer have a desire to do the same things, but if in the infancy of their salvation, they do not change environments, they can find their Christianity infected, retarded, or nonexistent at all. This process is not just seen in the lives of those without Christ. This process, at some point, reveals itself in all of us, in every dimension of our lives. Sometimes this divine discontent will show up in a relationship, a career, a ministry, or business. Regardless of where it shows up, the process is the same. Let us consider a passage of scripture.

> *1 And the sons of the prophets said unto Elisha, Behold now, the place where we dwell with thee is too strait for us. 2 Let us go, we pray thee, unto Jordan, and take thence every man a beam, and let us make us a place there, where we may dwell. And he answered, Go ye. (2 Kings 6:1-2)*

This is one of my favorite stories. The sons of the prophets, which literally means they were students of the prophets. These were prophetic mentees, being trained to serve, walk in, and move in the prophetic office. One day the school of prophets, under the pressure of an old season, declared the place was too "strait" for them. The word "strait" means small or narrow. Now we don't know if they grew numerically to the point where the location could no longer sustain them. This is possible, but I think there is a principle we can pull from this. Comfortability can sometimes be the worst enemy to a great leader. Moses was born, and hidden for three months. After he could no longer be hid, he was put in a basket, and tossed into a river. Jesus was born in a barn. Great leaders thrive in uncomfortable places. I believe these prophets had a palate change. This school was experiencing an appetite shift. Let's look at the process. After they announced that the place they were in was too small for them. Before we continue, I believe you need to announce that the place you're in is too small for you. Can you do that? Repeat this declaration out loud now:

Father, the place where I dwell is too small for me. I want more, I need more, and I decree that my capacity is expanding now. Give me the ability to hold more, do more, know more, manage more, lead more, make more, see more, hear more, and learn more. The season I am in has expired, and better is waiting for me now. I am growing by leaps and bounds, and my current situation can no longer sustain me. In Jesus name, Amen.

Now after they announced this, they said, "let us go to the Jordan." An appetite change demands a location change. It is only when you become so discontent with where you are that you are willing to step out. This is the power of the empty belly. God cannot allow some of us to become satisfied. Satisfaction would destroy us. Satisfaction would snuff out any hope of us reaching beyond the boundaries our doing something different. Do you think your discontent is because you do not have enough money? I want you to know that your discontent has been given by divine design so that you never get satisfied with what is possible. Whenever your palate has an upgrade, it is very hard for you to come back. When I was young, I remember having chicken seven times a week. When I began to work, and afford to buy my own food, I had an expensive taste. Even now I consider myself a foodie. I love trying out new restaurants. In all this exploring I did not notice that my appetite had shifted dramatically. It was only until I was offered fast food, which I denied with disgust, that I knew my palate had been promoted. Have you ever been there? Maybe it wasn't food, but a particular clothing style or designer. For you, it could've been shoes that became the identifying factor that you had reached a new place of maturity. For these young prophets, it was location. They could no longer stay where they were. Their request was to go to the Jordan.

The Jordan is a very symbolic place. If we remember, after Joshua was installed as the new leader of Israel, him and the Levites crossed the Jordan into the Promised Land. The Jordan River was the place that Jesus was baptized and inaugurated into His earthly ministry. The Jordan has always been a place that represented transition. The Jordan doesn't just represent locational transition, but divine transition. The Jordan signifies to us that we are at a watershed moment in our lives. The Jordan means that we are about to experience something that will inevitably change us forever. I believe you are at that point in your life. I believe that your reading this book signifies something more. You are crossing the Jordan. An appetite change is followed by a location change. For the sons of the prophets, this location change was geographical, for us it may be vocational. Sometimes the change from the ordinary to the extraordinary is spiritual, financial, or even emotional. Many times our Jordan is letting go of an old relationship, or a repeatedly disappointed expectation. Sometimes even the relinquishing of our own dreams becomes the Jordan we need to cross in order to enter the will of God. These prophets were hungry for something more, and that is where we are. We have reached the edge of the Jordan.

We're no longer satisfied with the meals of men. We want the impossible. If you can cook it, we don't want it. If you can think it, is not enough to fill my belly. Situations such as these are important for leaders. Moments such as these, when nothing around you seems to hit the spot, create in us a hunger for something more. Great men and women are identified by their appetites. Men and women of great feats are usually revealed by their desire to do what has never been done before. Is this you? Are you content with what has always been? I don't think you are. If you were, you would not be on the journey you are on now. You want more.

Now back to John Chapter 4. I love the question that the disciples ponder and pose to each other in verse 33, "has any man brought him something to eat." There is a level of fulfillment that people cannot give you. When you are on a mission, people cannot feed you. When you are headed towards a goal, the only thing that can satisfy you is to complete it. Hunger is powerful. The hunger that Jesus had leads Him out of Judea into a city known for idol worship. The hunger that Jesus had could not be extinguished by physical food. Men could not satisfy His desire to complete His assignment. We must be careful when our hunger for the validation of men outweighs our hunger to see God pleased. We must be hungry for God. Jesus makes an amazing statement. He says, "my meat is to do the will of him that sent me, AND to finish his work." When Jesus says "my meat" His is speaking of food. Food is the fuel of the body. Without food our bodies would lose strength, shut down, and eventually die. Jesus is juxtaposing His hunger with the hunger of the disciples. The disciples were physically hungry. In fact, they were so hungry, that they were willing to travel to another town to get food. Their physical hunger, and appetite, blinded them from seeing the harvest right before their eyes. The real harvest was not in the next town, it was in Samaria. Could it be that our physical hunger has stopped us from seeing the true harvest? We are so hungry for the things of the world that it has distracted us from our assignment. It seems as if this is the state of the church. We are the disciple traveling near and wide to find satisfaction, while Jesus is just sitting down waiting for us to return. We are so hungry with our own immature ambitions that we fail to see the great work that God wants to do right before our eyes. Our appetites have a way of leading us away from God. One thing that is great about Jesus is that He never leaves. He is patient in waiting for us to return.

Jesus says, "My meat is to do the will of him who SENT ME," this denotes assignment. If Jesus was sent, that means that there was a beginning to His journey and there was an end to His journey. Jesus was on an assignment. It was this assignment that leads Him to Samaria. It was this assignment that made Him go without food when everyone else could eat comfortably. Has your assignment ever made you uncomfortable? Planting Churches is not a hobby. Church Planting is an assignment. It has a beginning and an end. Have you ever started something, which was so important, that you could not stop until it was completed? This is the burden of completion. Once you begin something, it is hard to find satisfaction in anything else you do without that assignment being completed. It is not just satisfying to do the will of the Father, but to see His work completed. It is this hunger, this desire, which kept Jesus focused. We need leaders like that. Leaders that are willing to risk it all to do the impossible. Leaders that are not hirelings, just looking to get paid, but are willing to go to great lengths to see Jesus smile. We need leaders whose bellies are empty, dissatisfied with the diet of religion and the buffets of men. We need leaders who won't stop until the job is done.

The disciples by now have managed to surmise that Jesus has not physically eaten, but has a level of fulfillment because of the life changing encounter He has had with the Samaritan woman. His level of satisfaction baffles them. How can He get so much out of such a seemingly insignificant moment? One thing that I have learned about great leaders is that great leaders are able to perceive the power in every moment. Mature ministry is marked by the ability to discern moments. Every moment is not the same. Your aptitude to assess the moment gives you incredible value as a leader. This is a dimension of wisdom. Jesus personifies this perfectly. And like Jesus always does, He begins to speak to the heart of the issue.

> *35 Say not ye, There are yet four months, and then cometh harvest? Behold, I say unto you, Lift up your eyes, and look on the fields; for they are white already to harvest. (John 4:35)*

Jesus almost seems to veer off into a strange direction. It appears that Jesus is having a conversation underneath the obvious conversation. Jesus says "don't say that there are four months, and then a harvest." When Jesus says, four months, He is referring to what we know as a season. A season is the usual time it takes for a seed to die and bring forth fruit. Jesus gives His disciples a command. Now this is important to understand, we are about to have our faith stretched in an incredible way. I believe what Jesus was saying is that we are not bound by seasons. Seasons are not to control us; we are supposed to control the season. Can I prove this? I sure can. There was a prophet in 1 Kings 17 by the name of Elijah that commanded the Heaven to shut up and give forth no rain. Elijah, by his words, changed the season in a region.

> *17 Elias was a man subject to like passions as we are, and he prayed earnestly that it might not rain: and it rained not on the earth by the space of three years and six months. 18 And he prayed again, and the heaven gave rain, and the earth brought forth her fruit. (James 5:17-18)*

This verse of scripture makes me feel like a superhero. The Bible is very clear that Elijah was a human being. Elijah wasn't special, in the sense that he had something we don't have. Elijah was just like you and me. That should give us so much hope and faith. This scripture shows us that Elijah commanded that there would be no rain, and there was no rain. Now, let me stretch your faith for just a second. Maybe you skipped over it, because I did for many years. This verse does not say that it didn't rain, it says "and it rained not on the earth." WAIT A SECOND! You mean to tell me for three years and six months, not one drop of water fell on the planet? Look at the power of Elijah. How did Elijah do this? Elijah did this by prayer. And just in case you thought it was a coincidence, he prayed again, and the heaven gave rain. Elijah was a powerful gift.

Jesus commands us to not say that we are subject to seasons. Seasons come, and seasons go. God manufactures seasons for the purpose of growth and cultivation. Jesus is trying to communicate to the disciples that what you are waiting for, is actually waiting for you. Jesus says, "lift up your eyes," which is to say, "Open your eyes, for the harvest is ready." The disciples traveled miles away for a physical harvest, while the real harvest was right before them.

> *37 And herein is that saying true, one soweth, and another reapeth. 38 I sent you to reap that whereon ye bestowed no labour: other men laboured, and ye are entered into their labours.*

The disciples were so busy trying to feed their flesh that they missed the harvest. Jesus said that the harvest is already ripe. Your city is ripe. Your region is ripe. Your communities are ripe waiting for you to take the sickle of sacrifice and harvest what has blossomed in your area. Jesus then continues to tell them a truth. Whenever Jesus identifies that what He is about to say is true, we should listen intently. The scriptures say that Jesus is the Way and the Truth. Jesus doesn't have truth, He is Truth. When Jesus says that this particular saying is true, He is telling us that this is a principle. Jesus is about to share is a law that is unchangeable. The principle is this, one man sows, and another man reaps. We often have the audacity to think that we have arrived to our current place of success by our own efforts. There are times where we can become so prideful to think that we got to where we are alone. This is far from the truth. We are all the product of someone else's prayers. Jesus says that other men labored, and now we've entered into their labor. We literally stepped into the prayers of those that went before us. This is why empty bellies are so important. The discomfort of being hungry pushes us into dependency.

God wants us to depend on Him. God uses pain. I didn't say that He causes pain, but uses it, to push us out of our comfort zones. I believe with my whole heart that a lot of the pressure we feel is actually the prayers of our predecessors pushing us into the promise of God for our lives. Before we ever arrived on the scene, someone was praying for us. Decades before we got to our cities, the knees of leaders were flattened as they prayed for revival to become a reality within our neighborhoods. We have entered their labors. The harvest that the Church is about to see comes from years of fathers and mothers in the faith interceding on behalf of our nation. This was Jesus' answer to the harvest.

> *2 Therefore said he unto them, The harvest truly is great, but the labourers are few: pray ye therefore the Lord of the harvest, that he would send forth labourers into his harvest. (Luke 10:2)*

The harvest in our cities is truly great, but as Jesus said, the laborers are few. Do you know why? The laborers are few because they have all taken a trip to the nearest town to satisfy their flesh. When leaders are concerned with themselves more than they are with the harvest, cities miss moments of visitation. Could your city be missing a visitation from Jesus because you are too busy trying to feed yourself? Jesus gives us an answer to this problem. Jesus says, pray. Jesus tells His disciples that the solution to the lack of laborers is prayer.

CLEAR EYES

Prayer is a dynamic technology that we have as Christians. We understand prayer as communication with God, and it is, but prayer is so much more than that. Prayer is power. Prayer is a weapon. Prayer is the strategic pulling down of Heaven into Earth. Let us look at what is commonly referred to as the Lord's Prayer.

> *9 After this manner therefore pray ye: Our Father which art in heaven, Hallowed be thy name. 10 Thy kingdom come. Thy will be done in earth, as it is in heaven. 11 Give us this day our daily bread. 12 And forgive us our debts, as we forgive our debtors. 13 And lead us not into temptation, but deliver us from evil: For thine is the kingdom, and the power, and the glory, forever. Amen. (Matthew 6:9-13)*

We refer to this as the Lord's Prayer. I like to call it the Pattern Prayer. Jesus is giving us a format more than He is a script. This is not something that we repeat because of tradition, but a guideline that we use to structure our communication. I believe the core of this prayer is found in verse ten. "Thy Kingdom come. Thy will be done in earth, as it is in heaven." This is what prayer is. Prayer is not asking God for things. While there are times for this, that is elementary prayer. Prayer is the systematic establishing of God's will in the Earth. God's will is His desires, plan, agenda, works, and mind. Now when we understand this, prayer takes on a new meaning. Prayer, with this understanding, can no longer be something we only do before bed. This definition pushes prayer out of the realm of religious duty. Prayer becomes a lifestyle when we understand its purpose. Prayer was never intended to be an exercise. Prayer was engendered to be a constant two-way communication device that perpetually keeps us in sync with God's plan. Prayer is not something that we do, it is who we were. This brings clarity to the words of Jesus.

> And he spake a parable unto them to this end, that men ought always to pray, and not to faint; (Luke 18:1)

Even Paul said something that seemed ridiculous.

> Pray without ceasing. (1 Thessalonians 5:17)

I always thought that prayer was an enormous task. It seems as if this verse was written for super Christians. Throughout my prayer life, I have always endeavored to get to the point where I could literally pray without ceasing. This seemed like an impossible task, until I realized that prayer was not words. Now, we understand that prayer is the power of request, but it is not limited to that. Prayer, again, is the strategic pulling down of heaven to the earth. This is done many ways. This can be accomplished through song, dance, and even the planting of churches. Worship and prayer is like the respiratory system in the life of the Christian. Worship is us breathing in, and prayer is us breathing out. Prayer is an essential discipline in the life of the believer. But, let's be honest, prayer seems to be a lost art.

I am shocked to find out that most Christians do not pray. We bless our food, we pray for peace during rush hour, but for the most part, many of us are guilty of an infantile prayer life. Intercession is very important to the development of a church, and its leader. A leader that does not pray is not fit to lead. Communication is key. Nothing survives without communication. Relationships will die, businesses will fail, and churches will crumble when communication is not viewed as priority. Your prayer life is directly connected with your capacity.

I FEEL THE BURDEN

When I first accepted my call to preach, I had a difficult time. I had just come off the streets from being homeless. I was the new guy, in a new city, and even scarier, I was in a new church. I didn't know anyone, and kept to myself a lot. My first few years of ministry, I was lonely. My first few years of ministry were marked with intense depression and loneliness. I was prideful, so I never told anyone. If I could do it over again, I would have told my pastor. If you are reading this and you feel this way, you should definitely find someone to be accountable to, it will save you years. That time in my life really pushed me into prayer. God has ways of making us pray. Ask Peter! You haven't heard a prayer until you are about to drown. The waves of life are crashing into you, and the only thing you can scream is "HELP!" This is what this time was for me. During my alone time, I became acquainted with God in a way I could've never experienced if I was a part of the crowd. Many nights I fell asleep crying. I soaked my pillows for years asking God "why me?" The burden I felt to preach, minister, and build was extraordinary. At times I felt like I couldn't breathe because of the visions I saw of great churches being raised up and phenomenal preachers setting ablaze a generation of warriors. Soaked pillows became my badge of honor, my mark of distinction, and the validation of my rank.

Church planters need to have a burden for the Kingdom of God, their cities, and the people in their community. This weight of responsibility that the planter carries is dealt with by persistent, consistent, demonstrative and sometimes, even violent praying. Every seed needs water. Church planters provide the water with their tears. Our tears, during times of prayer, become the water to nourish the seeds that were sown by generations past. Here is an excerpt from a blog I wrote in August of 2012 entitled "WEEP FOR YOUR CITY"

> *"In January of 2011, something amazing happened to me. I prayed that the Lord would give me His heart for the city of Atlanta.. suddenly a burden came upon me, and I began to weep for hours. I couldn't stop weeping, and through intercession, I understood that what was taking place was something very sacred and precious. As I wept I began to realize that the seeds of revival that were planted by generations unknown*

to me were now being watered with the tears of a new generation that yearned to see what our fathers and mothers have so desperately prayed, cried, and even died for. In every city, great men and women have sown their lives to see their region established as a center for raw revival. Well my plea is for you to weep. Weep until you have no more tears and no more strength. Weep until you cannot stand, until you cannot help but believe that God is coming to your city.

Luke 19: 41 and when he was come near, he beheld the city, and wept over it.

When Jesus saw what Jerusalem missed as a result of rejecting him, He wept. Knowing what would come as a result. Our cities desperately need men and women that would weep for them. Our cities are crying out for revival, can you not hear it? We don't need another service, another religious center, another platform for powerless preachers... we need Noahs that would build REVIVAL in their back yard. We need Abrahams, who regardless of how barren their cities look, will continue to sow. We need Davids who would stop at nothing to bring the presence back to their city. We need Jesus to weep over our city. My plea to you is that you would fall in love with the destiny of your city... fall in love with it's purpose, with its future... and WEEP FOR YOUR CITY!!!"

Prayer must become the most important part of our journey. I implore you to pray that God gives you His mind for your city. Pray that God gives you His heart for your city. Prayer produces transfer. Whenever there is prayer, there is an exchange of power. Power shifts hands when you pray. Pray until God transfers the burden He has for your city unto your shoulders. Pray until you feel the weight and pressure of the responsibility for the destiny of your city. You must become a midwife to the destiny and purpose of your city. A church planter is more than someone who finds an area and gathers a group of people. A church planter is a kingdom agriculturalist with the mission to birth out the very plan of God in a region. How is this done? This is accomplished through prayer. Soaked pillows are a sign that a city's revival is close.

I believe God is calling for leaders who are not afraid to weep for their city. Weeping is a powerful tool of intercession. There are three types of tears that the human body produces. The first type of tears is called, Basal tears. These tears are always present. They exist to lubricate the eye, and are there so that our eyes never become dry. They help us to retain the flexibility of our vision. It allows us the comfort of looking in different directions without pain. Crying keeps us broken before the Lord, always in a place of evaluation. Evaluation is the key to perfection. You cannot become better if you are afraid to look at what you have produced from a different perspective. Basal tears give us the power of multiple perspectives, so that a panoramic view of our city and the state of the people can be understood. Basal tears combat religion. Religion has allowed our eyes to become dry, locking it into one perspective. When we look through the eyes of religion we can only see our city one way. We can only see it broken, fragmented and awaiting God's wrath. Basal tears give us the benefit of a different perspective. Basal tears gives us the privilege of seeing our city through the eyes of God, blessed, healed, whole, and awaiting revival to crash into it's shores.

The second type of tears is called Reflex tears. Reflex tears are the ones we desperately need. Reflex tears are activated to cleanse the eyes of dirt, debris, and other things that would hinder our vision.

> *3And why beholdest thou the mote that is in thy brother's eye, but considerest not the beam that is in thine own eye? 4Or how wilt thou say to thy brother, Let me pull out the mote out of thine eye; and, behold, a beam is in thine own eye? 5Thou hypocrite, first cast out the beam out of thine own eye; and then shalt thou see clearly to cast out the mote out of thy brother's eye. (Matthew 7:3-5)*

When Reflex tears are not present, our vision becomes blurred, and if not corrected, we could become blind. Reflex tears come to purify our way of seeing. These tears go to work whenever there is sin in our life. Sin hinders the way we see the world, God, and ourselves. Notice that the man in Matthew chapter 7 could not focus on anything in the other man's eye, but his deficiency. The sin in his own eye disabled him from seeing anything good in the man. Reflex tears are the tears of grace and mercy. What should have destroyed our vision was washed away. The Church needs reflex tears if we are going to see our cities and communities the right way. Let us throw away legalism, and believe God for great grace in our regions.

The last type of tear is probably the most commonly known tear; it's the Emotional tear. The journey of Emotional tears begins in the cerebrum where sadness is registered. Emotional tears are not just limited to sadness. There are many other emotions that produce tears. We've all had times of great joy, happiness, conviction, or compassion that produced tears. Emotional tears communicate something more than biological needs. Emotional tears are infused with the dealings of the heart. These tears have their own way of communicating our feelings and desires. It is these tears that hold so much weight during times of intercession and prayer. For a long time we have tried to separate our emotions from faith. I do not think this is possible or advantageous. Our faith should not be bound by our emotions but God did make us emotional beings. It is in the soulish realm of humans where the will, mind, and emotions are found.

> *And the very God of peace sanctify you wholly; and I pray God your whole spirit and soul and body be preserved blameless unto the coming of our Lord Jesus Christ. (1 Thess. 5:23)*

This scripture lets us know that as humans, we are body, soul and spirit. It is commonly explained this way; we are spirit, we have a soul, and we live in a body. God made us spirit beings according to Genesis chapter 1, verses 26 through 28. In Genesis chapter 2, verse 7; we see the body of Adam being formed by the dust on the ground. This is the formation of

Adam's flesh, or the shell he would occupy while on the Earth. In this same verse, God breathed into Adam's body the "breath of life" and Adam became a living soul. Adam became aware of himself. Adam was no longer just a spirit, or a body; he was now a living being. Adam was aware. It is this awareness that made Adam different from all other beings of the Earth. Adam knew his purpose, assignment, power, and authority. What a wonderful place of confidence and stability that must have been.

Our spirits connect us to God. Our souls connect us to us, and our flesh connects us to the world around us. Our flesh allows the world in through what we call gates. The five gates are our five senses: seeing, touching, smelling, tasting, and hearing. When the world comes through Adam's flesh, it is interpreted by Adam's soul. The soul is also the place of perspective and paradigm. Our soul begins being formed while we are yet in the womb. Our soul is shaped by our victories, failures, disappointments, and encouragements. Our soul is a powerful place. The soul is the seat of our emotions. Why are emotions so important to faith? Emotions, shaped by the human experience, bring passion to our faith. I was born and raised in Atlanta, and all the things that I have been through here, give me a unique perspective for my city. This perspective enables me to pray with a burden that only I can communicate. Think about the emotional attachment you have to the city you are in. Those attachments become the catalyst to chain breaking intercession that the demonic kingdom cannot compete with. Until we see our cities through the eyes of God, we can never truly be effective. This only happens through prayer.

Our tears have a language that even we sometimes cannot understand. Have you every felt like crying but did not know why? Have your eyes ever, without any warning, filled up with tears? This happens to me often. When I think of the city of Atlanta, my heart begins to break and tears begin to flow. This is a supernatural form of prayer. There are many different forms of prayer that we must be skilled in if we are going to bring deliverance to our city.

THE DIMENSIONS OF INTERCESSION

Intercession can be categorized into five sections:

1. Thanksgiving and Praise
2. Petition and Supplication
3. Proclamation and Decrees
4. Tongues and Mystery
5. Blessing and Impartation

Each one of these types of prayer holds a key to unlock the destiny of a city. Notice that I said previously that every leader must be "skilled" in these types of prayer. Prayer cannot just be viewed as an obligatory subject that we are forced to know. Prayer is a weapon that we engage willingly, in order to open our cities for God. Prayer opens cities. Prayer ripens regions. Prayer is the only legal way anything from Heaven has authority to enter the Earth. Nothing is permitted into the Earth until someone prays. We must pray, and pray earnestly, to contend for the soul of our city. Prayer is the technology of the Kingdom of God that OPENS HEAVEN, EXPANDS the CAPACITY of GIFTS, and RIPENS REGIONS for REVIVAL. Prayer turns the soil of a city and prepares it to receive the seed of the Kingdom. Now that we understand how important prayer is, let us look briefly into the types of prayer.

Thanksgiving and Praise

Thanksgiving and Praise may seem to be the most elementary and obvious form of prayer, but it is not. This type of prayer, honestly, is the most frequently ignored type of prayer. This is what the scripture says about thanksgiving and praise.

> *Enter into his gates with thanksgiving, and into his courts with praise: be thankful unto him, and bless his name. (Psalm 100:4)*

I won't spend too much time on the understanding of gates here; I will touch on that in the next chapter. It will suffice to say that gates are the place of business and transaction.

Every major marketplace in the days of old was positioned at the gates of the cities. Gates are places of exchange. This is what thanksgiving initiates for us. When we begin to thank the Lord, a divine transfer takes place. Thanking is a powerful concept. Have you ever done something for someone, and you saw how it blessed them? Maybe you remember the joy when you gave someone a gift, or the emotions they showed when you surprised them with an unexpected gift. Their very reaction gave you life. Their smile revealed their level of gratitude and it made you feel accomplished. When we receive that type of reaction, it makes us want to do things for those close to us, and sometimes even people we do not know. In the same stream of thought, have you ever done something for someone, and they did not show you gratitude? Have you ever given someone a gift, and they did not say "thank you?" Maybe they did not like the gift, and the level of their gratitude was very low. When someone doesn't show proper gratitude, it discourages one from feeling the need to do anything on their behalf.

Well, how do you think God feels when we don't enter His gates with thanksgiving? When the Bible says, "enter His gates," it is dealing with what I call the Protocol of His Presence. There is a way that we approach God, you always begin with thanksgiving. Thanksgiving is the right way to approach God. Entering into His gates literally means to come into God's presence. This must be irrespective of how you feel, what you think, or the day you've had. Thanksgiving must be consistent with what God has done, is doing, and what you believe He will do in the future.

Praise is a power source. Praise is literally a well of energy that the believer can draw from to cast off burdens and weights that slow us down.

> To appoint unto them that mourn in Zion, to give unto them beauty for ashes, the oil of joy for mourning, the garment of praise for the spirit of heaviness; that they might be called trees of righteousness, the planting of the LORD, that he might be glorified. (Isa. 61:3)

The scripture says that the garment of praise is the

antidote for the spirit of heaviness. Heaviness here is depression. Depression is an emotional burden that weights on our mind. When people are heavy, they lose motivation for life. Depression is a door to substance abuse, suicide, and is usually the root for procrastination. The Bible gives us the answer to this, and the answer is praise. Now this is when separating our emotions from our faith is useful. When one suffers with depression, or if they are distressed by the cares of life, it can be very difficult for them to praise God. Perfect praise requires our entire being to be engaged.

> Bless the LORD, O my soul: and all that is within
> me, bless his holy name. (Psalm 103:1)

The psalmist exhorts us to bless the Lord with our soul. The soul, again, is the place of our will, mind, and emotions. The psalmist continues by saying that everything in us should bless the Lord. We are to praise based on our potential, and not our problems. But how do I praise when I don't feel like it? How can I praise when my bills are past due? How can I praise when cancer is in my body. How can I praise when my church is not growing? Always remember that praise is not dictated by your circumstance. In actuality, it is praise that dictates your circumstance. Praise is contagious. We see this clearly at sports events. When your favorite athlete does something incredible, it is hard not to stand up and cheer, especially when everyone around you is yelling at the top of their lungs. Praise has the ability to jump from one person to another. The scripture says in psalm 100, and verse 4, that we enter the gates with thanksgiving, and into His courts with praise. The courts of the Lord are the place of judgment, favor, and legislation. Praise gives us favor in the courts of our God. The weapon of praise can deal with legal matters, court complications, and is a releaser of the favor of God.

Petition and Supplication

Now petition is the form of prayer we are familiar with the most. This is the power of request. Petition literally means to ask for something. While we are petitioning God, we are asking

for specific things. While petition is the most commonly
ιged form of prayer, it is also the easiest to mishandle.
/ing amiss, or missing your target in prayer, is easy during
?s of petition. To ask God for something requires you to
know what God desires to release. This is the secret to
petitioning God. If you ask for what God already has a desire to
see released, there is an explosion that takes place where you
enter the perfect will of God. In the perfect will of God, you can
ask want you want, and it will be done.

> *14 And this is the confidence that we have in him,
> that, if we ask any thing according to his will, he
> heareth us: 15 And if we know that he hear us,
> whatsoever we ask, we know that we have the
> petitions that we desired of him. (1 John 5:14-15)*

The word "confidence" means boldness in speech, open,
and frank utterance. The word "confidence" also means to
speak publicly, with full assurance and without ambiguity.
Petitions must be precise and targeted, otherwise we pray
without any result. James says it like this,

> *5 If any of you lack wisdom, let him ask of God,
> that giveth to all men liberally, and upbraideth not;
> and it shall be given him. 6 But let him ask in faith,
> nothing wavering. For he that wavereth is like a
> wave of the sea driven with the wind and tossed. 7
> For let not that man think that he shall receive any
> thing of the Lord. 8 A double minded man is
> unstable in all his ways. (James 1:5-8)*

James is not dealing with wisdom alone, this is a
principle. If you ask God anything, according to His will, He
gives it. God doesn't just give, when God gives, He gives
liberally. This is why we are to be generous givers, because
God is a generous giver. God will give His very last. Just ask
Jesus. Let us watch where James goes with this discourse.
James qualifies how we must ask. James says, when you pray,
you must ask in faith and nothing can be wavering. When we
pray for something we are not totally committed to seeing, we

have a promise that it will not happen. Wavering prayer happens when the will of God is not known. So what is the will of God for your city? The will of God remained a mystery to me for many years, even after I was born again. It was taught, and still is to this day, that the will of God is mysterious. The will of God always seemed, to me, like a big cosmic game of hide-and-seek. If I prayed and it didn't happen, I would relegate that prayer to the "not the will of God" section. This type of teaching and prayer life cancels the confidence of the Believer. Prayer is supposed to be passionate and confident. When the will of God is not known it causes Christians to cower in the presence of God, never truly tapping their real prayer potential. The will of God is not a mystery. The will of God is the mind of God. The will of God is the intent and desire of God. The mind of God is not a thing, but it is a person.

> *1 In the beginning was the Word, and the Word was with God, and the Word was God. 2 The same was in the beginning with God. (John 1:1-2)*

> *14 And the Word was made flesh, and dwelt among us, (and we beheld his glory, the glory as of the only begotten of the Father,) full of grace and truth. (John 1:14)*

The Bible says, unapologetically, that in the very beginning was the Word. Now we know that theologically the Word is Jesus in His pre-incarnate position. The word "Word" there in the Greek is *logos*. The word *logos* means intent, thought, a continued discourse, or sentence. Jesus was the complete sentence of God. All throughout the Old Testament, God spoke words that revealed His character and plan, but in the New Testament God speaks an entire sentence called Jesus. Jesus is the will of God walking. Jesus demonstrated the will of God perfectly and completely during His time on Earth.

> *And Jesus went forth, and saw a great multitude, and was moved with compassion toward them, and he healed their sick. (Matthew 4:14)*

And Jesus, when he came out, saw much people, and was moved with compassion toward them, because they were as sheep not having a shepherd: and he began to teach them many things. (Mark 6:34)

And when he was come near, he beheld the city, and wept over it, (Luke 19:41)

Jesus demonstrated the mind of God by showing compassion to the multitudes. The compassion of Jesus many times compelled Him to do incredible things. When we come to realization that Jesus is for us, and for our city, it will transform the way we pray for our region. Jesus was to invade your city will miracles, signs, and wonders. Just ask for it!

Proclamation and Decrees

Declarations must be made in every setting and during every occasion. When we make decrees we are revealing the will of God to the masses. It is one thing to understand that God wants to bring revival to our cities, it is another thing to stand up in the midst of people and declare "God is bringing revival to this city." When we make decrees we unify corporate assemblies to focus their prayer and attention to what has just been declared. This is an extremely potent form of prayer. Unified prayer or concert prayer is initiated by proclamations.

28 Thou shalt also decree a thing, and it shall be established unto thee: and the light shall shine upon thy ways. 29 When men are cast down, then thou shalt say, there is lifting up; and he shall save the humble person. (Job 22:28-29)

Job, which is the oldest book in the bible, reveals an ancient technology by saying, "thou shalt decree a thing, and it shall be established." The truth is solidified in the book of Genesis.

1 In the beginning God created the heaven and

the earth. 2 And the earth was without form, and void; and darkness was upon the face of the deep. And the Spirit of God moved upon the face of the waters. 3 And God said, let there be light: and there was light. (Gen. 1:1-3)

When there was no hope, and Earth was swallowed in darkness, God turned chaos around by a decree. Decrees are prompted by prophetic promises and inspiration. Declarations can be both spontaneous and systematic. We decree according to the promise of God over our lives. Churches that do not utilize decrees usually lack authority and definition within their prayer culture. We will deal with how to grow a culture of pray in the chapter *Greenhouses and Habitats.* When we decree within our churches, families and cities we are making known those things that we deem legal and illegal. Here are some declarations that you can proclaim over your city:

I decree that Jesus is Lord over this city, and His throne is established with power.
I declare that my city belongs to the Lord and is a magnet for the supernatural.
I decree that the soil of my city is ready and the Harvest is sure.
I declare that the curse of poverty, violence and dishonor is broken off of my city.
I proclaim that my city shall be known as a city of victory and triumph.
I decree that employment rise, and this city becomes an economic model.
I decree that Kingdom Centers are being raised up in our region.
I declare unity among pastors and leaders here.
I say that this city shall not die, but declare the works of the Lord. This city is the head, and not the tail. We are above and never beneath.

Why is decreeing important? We set the course of our affections when we decree publicly. Imagine if you are steering a giant ship. The bigger the ship, the harder it is to turn. Declarations are likened to the turning of the ship's wheel; even though you have turned it, it takes time for the ship to follow. This is why declarations must be consistent. Decrees are not just needed corporately, but also personally. Proclamations put a voice to your vision and steers you in the direction of your destiny.

Tongues and Mystery

> *26 Likewise the Spirit also helpeth our infirmities: for we know not what we should pray for as we ought: but the Spirit itself maketh intercession for us with groanings which cannot be uttered. (Romans 8:26)*

I will not take time to explain the baptism of the Holy Spirit, and it's need in the life of the Believer. I believe it can suffice to say that when we are born again we are given an incredible gift to communicate with God in a supernatural way. There are many times that the burden upon a leader is so heavy and inexplicable, that praying in the natural does not seem to render due benevolence. There are times where the things going on in our cities, and churches, will hide and disguise themselves. At these moments we have to forsake earthly languages and depend upon the Holy Spirit to pray through us.

In this dimension of prayer we also include weeping, travail, and birthing prayers. We spoke briefly about the power of our tears and the need for soaked pillows. Weeping is an invaluable asset to the human being. Travail and Birthing prayers still remain somewhat a mystery in the American church. If you are reading this book and you plan on planting a church, birthing prayers must become your best friend.

> *My little children, of whom I travail in birth again until Christ be formed in you. (Gal. 4:19)*

Paul, speaking to his spiritual sons and daughter in Galatia encouraged them that he was praying them through their trials. One of the jobs of a planter is to cultivate. To cultivate means to bring out. Another word for "bring out" is the word deliver. It is likened to a pregnant woman who is in full breach and now has to push. During those times of intense pain, it is hard for the mother to release anything intelligible. Many times during childbirth the only thing a mother can door is cry, moan and groan. This is the sound of travail. Now, even though those sounds don't mean anything to us, to God they are speaking wonderful things. The American church, for the most part, doesn't engage in this form of prayer because of our need to understand everything. I have come to find out that there are some things about God that will always remain a mystery. Mysteries are good. Mysteries develop our hunger, and instigate us to seek God on different levels. Mysteries mature our faith.

Blessing and Impartation

To bless literally means to speak highly of. We are to bless our city and not curse it. This form of prayer is most regularly seen before meals. Every time we sit done to eat, we pray over our food, believing that if there is anything harmful in it, it won't hurt us. Have you ever had to sit down and eat food you did not like? Or maybe you had a friend, who wasn't that good of a cook, prepare you a meal. Even when we do not like what is on our plate, we bless the food, we believe someone God can turn this meal around. We are to do the same thing with our cities and churches. We are to bless people. As a matter of fact, we are not just to bless, we are supposed to be a blessing. In the days of old, the responsibility of blessing was left to the father. When a father reached the zenith of his ministry and life, he would call his sons to him, they would kneel and he would lay hands on them. Blessing is best with impartation. A blessing is the pronouncement, but impartation is the power.

> By faith Jacob, when he was a dying, blessed both the sons of Joseph; and worshipped, leaning upon the top of his staff. (Hebrews 11:21)

The word "blessed" there means to cause to prosper. The word "bless" means to celebrate. The Greek word for bless is *eulogeo*. This is where we get the word eulogy. A eulogy is a speech or praise read for someone, usually when they're deceased. We are called to bless. Impartation is a form of prayer. Impartation is when there is intentional transfer from one individual to another through the channel of faith. Supernatural things take place when we believe God for impartation.

> *Neglect not the gift that is in thee, which was given thee by prophecy, with the laying on of the hands of the presbytery. (1 Tim. 4:14)*

Paul tells his son Timothy, do not neglect the gift that is in you. Sometimes we can become so busy building, that we forget we are truly anointed. Paul is very clear how Timothy received this gift. This was not something that he had at birth, nor was it something that he learned. Paul and the presbytery, through the laying on of hands, gave this to him. I love this about God. We are never at a disadvantage. If there is anything you do not have, you are one hand away from it. Impartation gives us the ability to share gifts and anointings.

All of these forms of prayer must be engaged if we are going to see churches grown and revival spread throughout our cities. Soaking our pillows is so important. It is only when we are willing to soak our pillows that God will release his flood over us. I admonish you; before you go to the next chapter, say this prayer aloud:

Lord, make my eyes intercessors. Give me a burden for my city. Arrest my heart, and give me the virtue of compassion so that I can see my city the way you see it. Lord, allow my heart to break for my city. I commit to fasting and prayer, worship and praise, until the floods of revival fill my city. I pray for unity. I pray for signs and wonders. I pray for miracles. Father, I know that your will over this city is to prosper and bless it. Make me a vessel of that impartation. In Jesus name, Amen.

FLOODS and EARTHQUAKES

Chapter Two

Priming Cities for Revival

The sun rises. Industrial giants reach for the sky. Cars begin their journey, and people begin their day. There is pollution, there is violence, but yet there is expectation. Crowded streets, billboards, street vendors fill the atmosphere with a nostalgic aroma making all of us feel just a little bit more comfortable. There are students, artists, the homeless, the executives . . . and the preacher. While ambient noises fill the air, tears fill the eyes of the preacher. His heart breaks, but his faith rises . . . he sees revival. He sees potential. He sees the prayers of pioneers. His tears, like prisms, mutate his vision into a dreamlike world . . . he believes. He believes that this city belongs to Jesus. He believes that Jesus wants so desperately to bring His love, His power, His Kingdom to such a place as this. God wants this city.

...These that have turned the world upside down... (Acts 17:6)

Do you feel that, there's a rumble, then a shaking, and a tumble. Breaking boundaries, take the city, ARE YOU READY, we're coming!!!

-Xstream, *Worship and Arts Department of Embassy*

I still remember when this song was first released in me and my wife's living room. For almost a year, a group of leaders and I would gather there to worship and pray, contending for the destiny of Atlanta. Every Sunday we would meet at six o'clock at night and push hard for the Kingdom of God to come in a fresh way to Atlanta. What if I told you that Jesus was waiting desperately to release revival in your city? What would you say if I told you that Jesus wanted to radically shake your city? I believe that cities are on the heart of God in this hour. You probably have already noticed that I have used the word "city" quite a bit. This is because if we are going to see transformation happen, we must plant in transformative areas. 21st century cities are the major engines of transformation in our time. If we are going to see impact and change, cities must be our target. WHERE we plant is just as important as WHAT we plant. Where we plant our churches is very important to God. Please understand that I am not speaking primarily about location, in terms of visibility, but location in terms of purpose and intent. Many times we plant churches in high traffic areas for the purpose of growth, never truly understanding the power of the city. Urban areas become a prophetic platform by which our churches have an opportunity to touch the world.

Gardening is the purpose of planting, growing, and cultivating plants. Gardening is also known as horticulture. Horticulture is the science, art, technology and business of planting, growing and cultivating plants. One who engages in horticulture is known as a gardener. A Gardener is a master planter. Those who have proficiency in planting are known as "green thumbs." Every gardener understands that the soil is just as important as the seed. Jesus gives us this understanding in the Parable of the Seed. This parable is very familiar. I like to refer to this parable as the Parable of the Soil.

> *1The same day went Jesus out of the house, and sat by the sea side. 2 And great multitudes were gathered together unto him, so that he went into a ship, and sat; and the whole multitude stood on the shore. 3 And he spake many things unto them in parables, saying, Behold, a sower went forth to sow; 4 And when he sowed, some seeds fell by the way side, and the fowls came and devoured them up: 5 Some fell upon stony places, where they had not much earth: and forthwith they*

sprung up, because they had no deepness of earth: 6 And when the sun was up, they were scorched; and because they had no root, they withered away. 7 And some fell among thorns; and the thorns sprung up, and choked them: 8 But other fell into good ground, and brought forth fruit, some an hundredfold, some sixtyfold, some thirtyfold. 9 Who hath ears to hear, let him hear. (Matthew 13:1-9)

Many times we call this parable the parable of the sower, or the parable of the seeds. But I think that these scriptures highlight the importance of the types of soil we plant in. Where we plant has an extreme effect on the health of our seeds. I am not saying that every church is called to the city. I believe God has a distinct and unique purpose for every kingdom center. You may be called to a small town, or to a rural area, but the principle is still the same. I think it is interesting to note here that most biblical cities were usually made up of a population of 3,000 people or less. Major metropolitan areas are not the only places we need churches, but I do believe there is a fresh emphasis on cities because of their dense population. Cities are the new frontier. As a church planter planting in the heart of a major city, I have noticed that because of zoning and other permit related issues, most churches are being forced out of the city because of a lack of real estate. This is demonic at its root. We need a generation of church planters that see this as a call to do the impossible. We must step out of the comfortable corners of suburbia, into the mean streets of the city. Where we plant our churches must be strategic. Every gardener understands that there are areas more conducive for growth than others. Before we go further, let me qualify growth in context. The growth we are speaking of now is not numerical growth. We will deal with that in a subsequent chapter. Our focus now is the health and development of a house.

PLANTING ZONES

Now in the planting world there are what is called Planting Zones. There are 11 planting zones on the USDA Plant

Hardiness Map in the contiguous United States and southern Canada. The regions are structured by a 10 degree Fahrenheit difference in the average annual minimum temperature. The higher the numbers, the warmer the temperatures for gardening in those areas. Planters must understand these areas and abide by their laws. For instance, a state like Florida is conducive for citrus fruit. States like Ohio and Michigan don't have the climate to sustain the growth for citrus fruits. Now Jesus, in the Parable of the Soil, gives us four distinct planting zones, only three of which produced any fruit. These are what I call, the planting zones of the Kingdom of God. The first place the seed falls is by the wayside. These are churches that are never truly planted. They begin, but without much preparation and thought, and are usually quickly devoured by the enemy. This is likened to anything we do for God without proper counsel and insight.

> For lack of guidance a nation falls, but victory is won through many advisers. (Proverbs 11:14 NIV)

Before we begin any God thing, we need to seek the proper information and advice. I know that you understand this, which is why you are reading this book. Without proper oversight we do not have sufficient insight, which leads to poor sight. There is a difference between planting a church and starting a church. I am not simply dealing with nomenclature, but I am addressing a trend. Planting churches requires preparation. Starting a church only requires inspiration. Inspiration without preparation usually leads to immature expiration. Starting a church denotes a finite journey. Anything that starts eventually has an end. When we plant, our focus is generational. Planting always begins with a seed, and ends with a seed for the next generation.

> And God said, Let the earth bring forth grass, the herb yielding seed, and the fruit tree yielding fruit after his kind, whose seed is in itself, upon the earth: and it was so.
> (Gen. 1:11)

Notice when God structured the Vegetative Kingdom, He made it self-sustaining. The Vegetative Kingdom was created with a seed within itself to produce another generation. We see this also in the Kingdom of Man. The Man, Adam, was a seed planted in the Garden (Gen. 2:15). But we also see that the seed of the Woman was in him. When God wanted to make Woman, He did not have to start from scratch. When God wanted to make Woman, He simply reached in Adam and grabbed a seed. When God wanted to make the child, we see this same process continued. The process was supposed to be organic. The process of planting begins with a seed, and it ends with a seed. This organic system of growth is the only true way to grow churches. One of the ways that churches fail before they start is by beginning prematurely. We have a culture of dishonor and self-promotion. We have grown a generation of leaders that want to start, but not be planted. Planting requires death. Planting requires selflessness. Starting connotes a race. This is what growing churches has become, a race to the proverbial top. We employ gimmicks, trends, and spend millions of dollars on marketing because we started something that never really had the endorsement of Heaven or our fathers.

Church planting was never supposed to be a race, but a journey designed to grow fruit, which has seed in itself, for another generation. Starting a church is very different from planting a church. Starting focuses on FINISHING, while planting focuses on FEEDING. Starting is centered on the RACE, which breeds competition. Planting is centered on the HARVEST, which breeds EXCELLENCE. Starting a church requires you to gather people who are attracted to the "movement." People will leave churches like this in the long run when they feel as if the "movement" has stagnated. When you plant a church you gather people who are attracted to the vision, which in turns produces a culture of service and sons. When you start a church you attract people who are fans of the gift, or people who want to do what you do, which breeds competition and jealously. You'll have an entire congregation of Absaloms serving only for position and favor. I know the word "starting" and "planting" are just terms, but terms formulate concepts, which become philosophies and eventually patterns of behavior. My goal is to challenge your understanding of what church planting was meant to be. We want to rescue church planting from the age of capitalism, and place it back in the hands of leaders who are burning with a passion to see the ways of revival flood their city. We can't afford to lose seeds. We lose seeds when we start something without the proper motives. This is why Jesus says that the seeds fell to the wayside.

The second planting zone in the Kingdom of God is stony ground. I parallel stony ground with rural areas. Rural areas are usually categorized as those places outside of the city limits. These places are usually farm areas and cannot be accessed without motor vehicles. Rural areas don't usually have public transportation, which limits jobs, economics, and many times population. Due to the dynamics of rural regions, it takes a certain type of church to grow in that location. Rural regions are more often than not comprised of family churches, which focus on community and accountability. Congregations in rural areas are mostly smaller, but because of the broad area of coverage, larger ministries can thrive here. Large churches grow well in rural areas because there is usually a lack of choices. Churches are scarce, everyone knows everyone, and so most communities attend the same church. Churches that are planted in rural places must focus largely on fellowship and teaching. One of the things that churches who plant in rural areas must be aware of is the tendency to preach exclusive doctrines. Churches that are in less dense population pockets tend to have less accountability and less competition. These churches can get away with false doctrine for years without ever being noticed because it takes a longer time for information to travel.

The third planting zone in the Kingdom of God is Suburban areas. These are close to the city, but are outside of the city. These areas get information quicker than rural regions, but can still be pretty slow in transformation. Suburban areas are community oriented and can be accessed many times without a motor vehicle, but usually don't have the benefit of public transportation. Due to the lower population density and the higher quality of residents, suburban areas make great places to live. Yet suburban areas are frequently home to very few jobs. Suburban employers tend to be "mom and pop" stores or community landmarks that have been in business for years. Suburbia makes for a great place to plant churches. This is the most popular place for church growth, because of the high visibility and population. Real estate in suburban areas is more expensive than those found in rural areas. There is a growing trend among Christians in America; people are beginning to travel less and less to attend a quality church. People are beginning to choose churches based on their proximity and not their purpose. This is a dangerous trend. Churches should never be chosen because of their closeness geographically, but their call globally. Churches must be chosen because of their vision and mission in an area. Our assignment as individuals must coincide with the assignment of the house we are planted in. This is necessary for us to have maximum impact and growth. This zone of planting is where the last generation of churches saw their greatest harvest, but the harvest is shifting.

Cities are the soil of the 21st century. The fourth and final zone of plating in the Kingdom of God is the city. The world is rapidly becoming more urbanized. As cities grow larger, our communities grow smaller as we see a swift integration of cultures, colors, and classes of people. Cities have become the fields of the 21st century, pregnant with an enormous harvest that the church can no longer ignore. Masses of people are moving out of rural towns as employment opportunities relocate and population weight is dramatically shifting. Population weight is a term I would like to introduce here. I will be introducing new ideas and terms throughout this book. Some are mine, and others come from people much smarter than me. Population Weight refers to the number of people in a given area. In a sport, such as wrestling, we use the phrase "throwing your weight around," which refers to ones ability to use physical weight, influence, and resources to get things done quicker. It is the same with an area's population weight. Cities are denser in population. So the production we see in cities, as it relates to ideas, creativity, revenue, and even culture, are much more potent than what we see in less populated areas. Cities are the engines of a nation. Highly populated areas have the ability to push laws and legislation, policies and propaganda, and even communication and culture at amazing speeds. Cities are the brain and nervous system of the nations of the earth. It is important that the Church understands the importance of cities if we are going to see revival hit our nation.

Cities are energy forces and strategic centers that are understood throughout the entire world. Everyone's eyes are focused on the cities of the world. Cities are drawing new interest and research based on the influence they carry to shift the destiny of nations. Cities carry with them a tremendous force of economic and cultural power, and have become the leading hub of all exchange, be it financial, creative or philosophical. We find all of the mind molders (Family, Government, Media, Arts and Entertainment, Business, Religion, and Education) in the city.

Thousands of people are converging on cities every year. There is a mass exodus happening all over the world. Now, to be global, means you only have to step outside of your front door. It is almost as if God has brought the nations to us. Where else do we see this happen?

> And when the day of Pentecost was fully come..
> And there were dwelling at Jerusalem Jews,
> devout men, out of every nation under heaven.
> (Acts 2:1,5)

Jerusalem was a capitol city. It was a popular metropolis that people from all nations would gather and celebrate the Feasts of the Lord and various Holy Days. All nations, at once, converged and descended on this city. It literally was a divine movement. God brought all the nations of the Earth to this once place to experience revival. This is what I believe God is doing with 21st century cities. Cities are becoming the platform for major transformation. I believe that since cities shape our regions, if we can shape our cities, we can impact our regions in a phenomenal way.

SHAPING OUR CITIES

The shaping of cities is an important thing. We are called to be city shakers and shapers. Every city has geography. Geography is the study of the physical features of the earth and its atmosphere, and of human activity as it affects and is affected by these. The same way that there is physical geography in a city, there is also spiritual geography. Spiritual geography is the spiritual make-up of a territory. Spiritual geography can be seen and discovered by a demographics study revealing how many different religious groups are represented in a neighborhood, and their population. Another way to determine the spiritually geography in your city is to identify the princes, or people of influence there. This can be harder, but beginning at the largest churches can be a good start. Large churches shape our regions in quite a significant way. Large churches hold much of the population in a given area, so there impact is felt at a quicker rate than the vibrations made in a smaller congregation. Spiritual geography can change as leaders fall and are raised up. The planting or uprooting of a church can have dramatic affects on the spiritual geography of a city.

Geography is molded and shaped by what we would term as natural disasters. Major storms and natural phenomena, such as tornadoes, floods, volcanoes and earthquakes have lasting effects on the geography of the earth. God has called us to be the molders of our regions. Through a flood of God's presence and the earth shaking power released through our worship and praise, our cities are shaped into centers of God's glory. Let's explore how we can do this strategically.

When we enter any region, there is a plan that God has for that place. Our role is to release the will of God wherever we are planted. Every region and city has dams that are designed demonically to keep the will of God inactive. Demonic dams exist to limit the flow of the power of God in a certain area. There are many different dams, but one of the most common dams is religion. Religion compartmentalizes God into eras and time spans. Religion makes God a tradition and not a living being that still has power to engage the "now." We serve a living God, who is interested in our "today." Our God is not locked in the past of tradition, but stands on the shore of our present waiting to do something amazing. Religion is a major dam that must be broken. Bad doctrine is another major dam that we must demolish. The dam of false doctrine has been constructed for years because of error. Doctrinal errors will always exist, but apostolic teaching can drastically decrease the extent and duration in which they are perpetuated. When I refer to apostolic teaching, I am not in any way referring to a denomination. When I say apostolic, I am dealing with the model set forth by the apostles of the scripture. The apostles set forth a tremendous pattern that produces power, if applied. The apostles taught very meticulously. They shared teaching with each other; they judged words and convened in apostolic councils in order to clarify teachings and positions. Demonic dams are designed to prevent floods. A flood of the love of God is exactly what we need. Dams have been erected in every arena of our society to keep the waters of God out. In order to flood our society, it is going to take an extreme amount of force . . . I call this, CONVERGENCE.

Convergence can be defined as the degree or point at which lines, objects, people, or ideas come together. In Computer Science, convergence is the combining of different forms of electronic technology, such as, data processing and word processing converging into information processing. Convergence is the combining of different forms of technology to increase the STRENGTH, POWER and INFLUENCE of the overall IMPACT. A move of God is waiting to converge in our cities. This convergence took place in Noah's day by the unlocking of the Heaven's and the wells. When the Heavens open, and the wells of our regions open, major things can take place in our cities. Let us first deal with the Heavens.

In the beginning God created the heaven... (Gen. 1:1)

The word "Heaven" here is the word *shamayim* in the Hebrew. This word literally means the atmosphere or the expanse in which the Universe was formed and placed. After God created the Heaven and the Earth, we understand that something happened. We don't want to spend time here building a theological case for what caused the Earth to be "without form and void" (Gen. 1:2), but we will say that the Earth was not created to be uninhabited (Isa. 45:18-19). Something happened that caused the Earth to become empty and desolate. God begins the recreative process by saying, "Let there be light." This begins a seven day creational process, which will bring power and order back to the Earth.

7 Creational Days- 7 Creational Systems (Each system produces something)
1. Greater Light and Lesser Light
2. Sky and Sea
3. Land and Vegetation
4. Sun, Moon and Stars
5. Fish and Birds
6. Man and Beast
7. Sabbath

On each day God does not just create anything, but He builds a self-sustaining system. Each day is a system replete with laws and functions. Day two is the day we want to look at briefly.

> And God said, Let there be a firmament in the midst of the waters, and let it divide the waters from the waters. And God made the firmament, and divided the waters which were under the firmament from the waters which were above the firmament: and it was so. And God called the firmament Heaven. And the evening and the morning were the second day. (Gen. 1:6-8)

UNDERSTANDING THE HEAVENS

The word "firmament" in verse six is the word *raqiya,* and it literally means expanse or space. On day one, God said, "Let there be light" and on day two, God said, "let there be space." Light demands space. Revelation demands a platform. Light must travel, or otherwise shadows are produced. When there is something blocking the release of light, shadows are inevitable. The Body of Christ has lived for generations on shadows. We have had so much in the way of our progress, but I believe we are in a new day. I believe this generation of leaders is going to see things we have never seen before. This is because our fathers had the courage to move that that was hindering light, out of the way. This is a powerful time for light. Space is created on day two. Whenever space is created, you have to

51

get excited, because there is coming something to fill that space. Losing something can be hard, but it is actually creating space. Church planter, you have to understand that you may have lost members, and even some leaders, but God had to make room for you, because He is about to fill you up.

Genesis chapter 1, verse 7, says something very key. In verse 7, the scripture says that the firmament separated the waters above from the waters beneath. When the heavens were created, it divided two bodies of water; the waters that were under the firmament and those above the firmament. I have heard many people speak on the waters above. Some speculate that the waters above helped to create a suitable atmosphere for the man to live in. Some say that this structure would have formulated a perfect atmosphere and environment for life to grow. This is what we call the "Greenhouse effect." We will go into detail about this in the chapter, *Greenhouses and Habitats.*

The word, *raqiya*, comes from the root word, *raqa*. *Raqa*, pronounced raw-kah, means to beat, stretch, or spread abroad. The heavens, or the firmament, was literally stretched or pulled like a curtain to cover the Earth.

> *Thus saith God the LORD, he that created the heavens, and stretched them out. (Isa. 42:5)*

> *..that stretcheth out the heavens as a curtain, and spreadeth them out as a tent to dwell in;*
> *(Isa. 40:22)*

Can you see this picture? God, like a painter, takes a canvas called the Heavens, and stretches it on the floor. The Master Painter is about to paint His finest piece. There is a structure in the Heavens. The Jews believed there were seven Heavens. Each heaven is guarded by a prince, or angelic commander. I really wish we had time to consider what the Rabbis taught, but I promise I will in another book. Paul taught that there were at least three heavens.

> *I knew a man in Christ above fourteen years ago, (whether in the body, I cannot tell; or whether out*

of the body, I cannot tell: God knoweth ;) such a
one caught up to the third heaven. (2 Cor. 12:2)

This has become a general teaching in the Body of Christ. I will use this template to clarify my thought. Every Heaven, or atmosphere, is created to contain particular things.

1. **First Heaven**- High Heavens- Planets and/or Galactic systems
Low Heavens- Fowls of the Air
2. **Second Heaven**- Fallen angels (principalities)
3. **Third Heaven**- The Realm of God

Let's look very quickly at the second heaven. It is the second heaven that we are contending for in our cities. It is commonly understood that the second heaven is the place of most spiritual activity. The second heaven is the battleground over our heads. The Bible says that Satan is the "prince of the power of the air" (Eph. 2:2). Satan seeks to rule the Heavens. He tried on one occasion to highjack the third heaven and was banished. Now he seeks to establish a pseudo kingdom within the second heaven. Our city's condition is only the manifestation of what is happening in the heavens. The pollution, violence, and decay of our cities reveal the warfare that is going on over our heads. Church planters must be acquainted with what is happening. I wrote a blog called "The Dynamics of Regional Princes" that explains this.
Look at this excerpt:

GUARDS OVER CITIES

We must, as apostles and as apostolic houses, understand the Angelic economy over our regions.

Dan. 10:20 Then said he, Knowest thou wherefore I come unto thee? And now will I return to fight with the prince of Persia: and when I am gone forth, lo, the prince of Grecia shall come.

This scripture shows us clearly that there are high

ranking angelic beings given rulership over nations and regions. These being are called PRINCIPALITIES or PRINCES, because they rule by PRINCIPLES. Principalities actually release PRINCIPLES over regions and people groups, and as these principles are promulgated and established, it becomes trends, and when those trends are sustained, it becomes strongholds of culture.

Let's look at how this works: ANGELS SQUAT OVER REGIONS
Principalities that are given custodianship over regions, literally SQUAT over these areas. We see this is Gen. 1.

Gen. 1:1 In the beginning God created the heaven and the earth.

Gen. 1:2 And the earth was without form, and void; and darkness was upon the face of the deep. And the Spirit of God moved upon the face of the waters. The word "moved" is "rachaph"- it means to brood, to incubate, and to sit on the earth as a hen sits on her egg. God literally SQUATTED over the Earth and began to give BIRTH. When Angelic Princes squat over a region, they begin to labor to produce and birth the destiny of that region. When Demonic Princes squat over a region, they actually release FILTH over that place. Squatting is an Apostolic Function. You see this in the ANIMAL KINGDOM. Animals such as lions and other large animals will enter a new territory and squat over that place. They will urinate or defecate there as a sign that "this is my territory."

Apostles are supposed to claim the rights of cities and regions. It is sad when "apostles" move into a city or region and the demonic powers don't even *take notice of him/her. We must move with such RANK, that all the cohorts of Hell begin to strategize our demise when they feel us coming.*

When an Apostolic Gift comes to a region, he/she brings a horde of angelic power with him. Let's look at this in a systematic way:

You have a city like Detroit. Unemployment, murder, sex trafficking, and drugs have raped the city. These Demonic Princes have squatted over that land and released that FILTH. So God raises up an APOSTOLIC GIFT. When that gift comes to town, he brings with him:

The Spirit of Invention to battle Unemployment. This raises Entrepreneurs.

The Spirit of Peace to combat Murder. This manifest in proactive children education programs, prison ministry, and the unification of churches to bring an atmosphere and image of peace in the city.

The Spirit of Holiness to war against Illicit Sexual Activity. This comes through the establishing of a standard among individuals first, then homes, then churches, and businesses.

The Spirit of MIRACLES, SIGNS and WONDERS to battle addiction to DRUGS and DRUG TRADE. The only thing that can break the power of a depressant, or a hallucinogenic, is the POWER of GOD.

Although that was lengthy, it is important for us to understand why the heavens cannot be ignored. There are STRONGMEN in the Heavens that we must battle and displace. The major spiritual influence in a region is called a STRONGMAN. A Strongman is appointed by what we call

Principalities. Satan's kingdom has a hierarchy. We find this in Ephesians chapter 6,

> For we wrestle not against flesh and blood, but against principalities, against powers, against the rulers of the darkness of this world, against spiritual wickedness in high places. (Eph. 6:12)

Principalities are princes that have been given rulership by kings. There are Godly princes, like Michael, the archangel, and Gabriel, the Revelation Carrier. There are also demonic princes. These princes rule over regions. I believe that over every city there sits a throne. That throne belongs to the dominant prince of that region. If the Lord Jesus is being exalted, and the Kingdom of God is advancing, churches are praying, and the Body of Christ is unified, Godly princes can occupy those thrones and set up godly strongmen. Equally, if the spiritual and moral condition of a city is rotting and decaying, them demonic princes gain control. This is one of the reasons God raises up churches, to displace demonic princes. Apostolic Houses, or Kingdom Centers, have a mandate to dethrone demonic authorities and bring revival to our regions.

> When a strong man armed keepeth his palace, his goods are in peace: (Luke 11:21)

Principalities come and lodge over regions. They become Lords of the airways. A Lord is one who is in charge of the distribution of goods. They will hold prosperity, health, and revelation captive.

> No man can enter into a strong man's house, and spoil his goods, except he will first bind the strong man; and then he will spoil his house. (Mark 3:27)

The Process of Principalities

1.**Principalities SET strongmen on Thrones in the Heavens.** (Release thoughts that are grabbed and embraced by Kings)
2.**Strongmen BUILD strongholds** (these are complex

structures that form the way a person thinks)

3.**Strongholds HOLD captive goods** (people, gifts and destiny)

One of the jobs of demonic princes is to close the Heavens. The term "closing the heavens" literally refers to the shutting down of a move of God, or moves of God, in a particular region. A closed heaven is a stale heaven. In 1 Kings 17, Elijah comes on the scene and announces that there will be "no rain or dew" for three and a half years. Well, when the heavens are shut up, a famine is produced in a region. In Elijah's day it was a physical famine, but in our day, it is a spiritual famine. When there is a closed heaven over our city, churches cannot grow because every seed needs water. An open heaven represents a time and space of immeasurable favor and blessing.

> And straightway coming up out of the water, he saw the heavens opened, and the Spirit like a dove descending upon him: (Mark 1:10)

When the heavens are opened over our cities, anointing, revelation, and miracles must happen. Open heavens require us to sow. John didn't just recognized the new season, which was Jesus, he sowed it. John sowed Jesus by baptizing him. Do you realize what John did? John planted Jesus, and a move of God was birthed in Judea. Planting is one of the ways to open the heavens. As we till the ground by fasting and prayer, something supernatural occurs . . . the heavens open!

DIG A WELL

Now let's look at the importance of wells. What is a well? A well was a watering place in the days of old. Wells were places of exchange. At times women would gather there to get water for their family. In John chapter 4 we see a woman coming to a well. All throughout the scriptures we will see women gathering at wells. In the book of Exodus, when Moses flees Egypt, and comes to Midian, he comes to a well and has to rescue the seven daughters of Jethro. Wells are always places of warfare. Wells represent wealth and ingenuity. Whoever controlled the wells, controlled the wealth of the region. Wells were used to water flocks and small pockets of vegetation. If a church is going to grow, it will need open wells. Wells are:

1. A place of generational supply
2. A place where wombs gather
3. A place where deposits are given

> For all the wells which his father's servants had digged in the days of Abraham his father, the Philistines had stopped them, and filled them with earth. (Gen. 26:15)

In the days of Isaac, the Philistines would fill the wells with dirt in order to shut down the economy of a region, and destroy the legacy of Abraham. The enemy is looking to destroy the generational wells of water in our cities by tarnishing the reputation of spiritual giants and fathers. Every time one of our leaders fall, whether it is by lack of integrity, or demonic attack, wells of revival are stopped up.

> And Isaac digged again the wells of water, which they had digged in the days of Abraham his father; for the Philistines had stopped them after the death of Abraham: and he called their names after the names by which his father had called them. (Gen. 26:18)

Church planters, we must be guilty of re-digging the wells in our city. There are many revivals and moves of God that have taken place in our city. The power of those moves is waiting to be harnessed and harvested. We cannot think that we are going to see great success without connecting to the power of the past. A well is a place where wombs gather. In the days of old, wombs were women, but now it represents anyone who has the ability to be fruitful. Every leader is a womb waiting to be impregnated with purpose. Our churches must be a well of power, information, anointing, and purpose. When the wells of the city, or the churches, are stopped up with filth, people will eventually leave. People cannot stay in a place where they are not getting nourishment.

> And it came to pass after seven days, that the waters of the flood were upon the earth. In the six hundredth year of Noah's life, in the second month, the seventeenth day of the month, the same day were all the fountains of the great deep broken up, and the windows of heaven were opened. And the rain was upon the earth forty days and forty nights. (Gen. 7:10-12)

This is what we call convergence. The flood of Noah's day was caused by the "fountains of the great deep" being broken, and the "windows of heaven" being opened. There was a convergence of the waters above and the waters beneath. As church planters and leaders pray earnestly, rending the heavens, and establishing wells of refreshing by planting churches, there is a convergence that is waiting to hit our cities. In Noah's day, the flood changed the landscape of their generation. There is a move of God waiting to transform the landscape of ours as well. It is going to take selfless men and women who are willing to open the heavens and dig some wells. Floods are violent. Floods have the ability to displace homes, and upset entire nations.

> For the earth shall be filled with the knowledge of the glory of the LORD, as the waters cover the sea. (Hab. 2:14)

DO YOU FEEL THAT?

Floods, with their mighty waves, shape the earth violently. Another natural occurrence that has rocked the earth, reshaping its landscape, is earthquakes. Most of us have heard of the San Andreas Fault, which runs through the state of California in the United States. A fault is a planar crack in a rock along which slippage has taken place. Some faults are small, almost microscopic; others are huge, like the one in California.

These faults can become huge contributors to earthquakes. In 1906, California was shook by a historic earthquake, now known as the San Francisco Earthquake of 1906. On a Wednesday morning at 5:12 a.m., April 18th, 1906, California would be forever changed. Earthquakes can remodel futures and renovate destinies. All of us have been victims of earthquakes. Maybe not physically, but perhaps emotionally, psychologically or even relationally. The 1906 earthquake killed 3,000 people, and over 80% of San Francisco was destroyed. This earthquake has been categorized as one of the worst natural disasters in the history of the United States. God has called us to create earthquakes in our cities. God has called us to be city shakers. We are to be reformers and molders of society. Causing a spiritual earthquake takes much force and power. As city SHAKERS we disrupt the equilibrium of the city, making sure all demonic powers are off balanced and have no power.

An earthquake, or tremor, is caused by a sudden release of energy in the Earth's crust, which creates seismic waves. The seismicity or seismic activity of an area refers to the frequency, type, and size of earthquakes experienced over a period of time. When was the last time your city was shaken for God in a notable way? Can you remember the last time there was a major move of God in your city? We are called to create earth shaking moves of God that generations to come will remember. We are not to build forgettable churches, but churches that leave such an impact and imprint in our cities, that they will affect generations unborn. Let's look at how we create earthquakes.

Every world is structured like a house. When I use the term world, I do so loosely. The word "world" here can represent any structure built with intent or design. The world that we live in is built by design. Our world, or society, has supportive pillars. These pillars are: Government, Family, Education, Religion, Business and Finance, Arts and Entertainment, and Media and Technology. We know these pillars as the Seven Mountains or Mind Molders.

And Samson took hold of the two middle pillars upon which the house stood, and on which it was borne up, of the one with his right hand, and of the other with his left. And Samson said, Let me die with the Philistines. And he bowed himself with all his might; and the house fell upon the lords, and upon all the people that were therein. So the dead which he slew at his death were more than they which he slew in his life. (Judges 16:29-30)

Samson caused an earthquake by pushing on the pillars. As we push on the pillars of society, we cause earthquakes in our city, but there is a risk. Samson died as a result, and we too must not be afraid to lose our life to see real transformation in our regions. It may be the death of our popularity, the death of our reputation or our actual lives, but if we are going to transform the spiritual geography of our cities, this is the price. Like Samson, these pillars surround us, and we interact with them on a daily basis. Planting churches requires us to address, with boldness, the society in which we live. A church that is irrelevant is not needed. As city shakers, we are called to apply pressure to the pillars of the world we live in.

Our Earth is divided into three sections: the core, the mantle, and the crust. The core itself is made up of two sections called the inner core and the outer core. The Mantle is the thickest section of the earth. The Mantle is the location of the hypocenter and is known for what is called convention currents. The Mantle is made of molten rock, that when under pressure, can be released by breaking through the earth's crust. We know this as Volcanoes. Convention currents are like the currents of the ocean, but instead of moving within water, these flows of direction move within molten rock. The movement that we see in convention currents is caused by the difference in temperature. The closer one is to the core, the hotter the temperature, which results in more movement. The further one is from the core, the cooler the temperature, which results in less movement. The core represents the headship of a ministry. It represents the senior pastors and usually the executive staff. We will deal with this in depth in the next chapter. The Mantle represents the leadership. It is interesting to note that the closer people are to you, the hotter the heat. This is true of ministry. Many times people think that the closer they are to the pastor, the better life will be, this is not true. The closer you are to headship, the more hell you will have to go through. The closer you are to the pastor, the more pressure and responsibility you carry. Being close to the headship is a dangerous position and privilege and must be revered and honored. The crust is the section of the earth we are most familiar with. The crust represents the fellowship of your church. The crust is the place of fruit and production, and usually is the most affected section during an earthquake. When there is an earthquake in your church, even if it is underneath the surface, hardly felt or registered on the Richter scale of your church, you can tell by the way it affects the fellowship. When people leave your church, there has been an earthquake somewhere. Some earthquakes are good, others can be destructive.

HYPOCENTERS and EPICENTERS

When we are dealing with earthquakes, and how to shake our cities for God, we have to deal with and understand the function and difference between hypocenters and epicenters. Every earthquake has a hypocenter and an epicenter. An earthquake's hypocenter is the position where the strain energy stored in the rock is first released. This position marks the point where the fault begins to rupture. This occurs at the focal depth below the epicenter. Beneath every epicenter, there is a hypocenter. The term hypocenter also refers to the point on the Earth's surface directly below an atmospheric explosion. Within the dynamics of earthquakes, a hypocenter is the point of power. The epicenter is where the power is first seen, but the hypocenter is where the power is first released. We don't want to just be an epicenter, but we want to become a hypocenter for the earthquake that is going to shake our city. What produces this power? The hypocenter is the site of the initial explosion. This happens underneath the surface where no one can see. The hypocenter is the work that no one else sees except you are your core team. The hypocenter is all the prayer, planning, hours of tears and arguments. It is the giving, worship, and digging you did before you planted your church. The hypocenter is the years of obscurity and service that you put in before you ever launched. The hypocenter is the place of true power. Without a hypocenter, the earthquake does not have lasting impact.

The epicenter is very important as well. The epicenter is the point directly above the true center of disturbance, from which the shock waves of an earthquake apparently radiate. The epicenter is the focal point of activity and/or the absolute center of something. Every church must become an epicenter for an earthquake. The force released in the hypocenter will determine the force of the earthquake in that city. Every earthquake has shock waves. The shock waves are the vibrations created as an effect of the release of energy that happens during an earthquake. A shock wave is a type of propagating disturbance. Like an ordinary wave, it carries energy and can propagate through a medium (solid, liquid, gas or plasma) or in some cases, in the absence of a material medium, through a field such as, the electromagnetic field. A shock wave creates pressure. Pressure is an effect, which occurs when a force is applied on a surface. Pressure is the amount of force acting on a unit area. Earthquakes are known by their pressure. In the world of earthquakes, there are different sizes. Earthquakes are known for their sizes, which are determined by their destructive power and their area of coverage. We are called to cause earthquakes. There are several occasions in the scripture when the earth quaked.

1. When Solomon was anointed.

So Zadok the priest, and Nathan the prophet, and Benaiah the son of Jehoiada, and the Cherethites, and the Pelethites, went down, and caused Solomon to ride upon king David's mule, and brought him to Gihon. And Zadok the priest took an horn of oil out of the tabernacle, and anointed Solomon. And they blew the trumpet; and all the people said, God save king Solomon. And all the people came up after him, and the people piped with pipes, and rejoiced with great joy, so that the earth rent with the sound of them. (1 Kings 1:38-40)

The Bible says that when Solomon was anointed, the earth was rent. Whenever there is an anointing released, there is a shaking.

2. When Jesus died.

And, behold, the veil of the temple was rent in twain from the top to the bottom; and the earth did quake, and the rocks rent; (Matt. 27:51)

3. When Jesus rose from the dead.

And, behold, there was a great earthquake: for the angel of the Lord descended from heaven, and came and rolled back the stone from the door, and sat upon it. His countenance was like lightning, and his raiment white as snow: And for fear of him the keepers did shake, and became as dead men. (Matt. 28:2-4)

4. When Goliath fell, the Earth did shake.

Goliath was so massive, that when he fell, I believe there was an earthquake. Whenever a giant falls, be it a demonic principality, or a Godly man or woman, the earth trembles.

5. Joshua and the Barrier Breakers.

Now Jericho was straitly shut up because of the children of Israel: none went out, and none came in. And the LORD said unto Joshua, See, I have given into thine hand Jericho, and the king thereof, and the mighty men of valour. And ye shall compass the city, all ye men of war, and go round about the city once. Thus shalt thou do six days. And seven priests shall bear before the ark seven trumpets of rams' horns: and the seventh day ye shall compass the city seven times, and the priests shall blow with the trumpets. And it shall come to pass, that when they make a long blast with the ram's horn, and when ye hear the sound of the trumpet, all the people shall shout with a great shout; and the wall of the city shall fall down flat, and the people shall ascend up every man straight before him. (Josh. 6:1-5)

When Joshua and the children of Israel marched around Jericho, I believe the earth shook. It was this shaking, combined with their corporate cry, that brought the walls down. If we are going to cause an earthquake in our cities, that will rearrange the very spiritual geography of our regions, we must engage in corporate prayer and worship. Are you ready to shake your city?

Shoulders and Soldiers

Chapter Three

How to Build a Power Team

MODERN DAY NOAHS

God is looking for modern day Noahs. God is searching for men and women that will build revival in their cities. Revival is not something that happens, it is a culture that is built systematically. Understand that revival is the true purpose for planting. Our purpose for planting is to refill, and refilling always revives a territory. This is what Noah did. Noah is a phenomenal model and pattern of a planter. As a matter of fact, the scripture calls Noah a planter.

And Noah began to be an husbandman, and he planted a vineyard: (Gen. 9:20)

That word "husbandman" is the word *adamah* in the Hebrew. *Adamah* literally means the ground. It is where we get Adam from, because Adam was made from the ground. Noah was skilled at working with dirt. Noah was not afraid to get dirty. When you work with people, you are going to get dirty. I believe this is one of the reasons God chooses the vessels that He chooses. When you look at the life of Noah, Abraham, Moses, David, and Jesus, these men were not afraid to get dirty. Jesus on one occasion washed the feet of His disciples. Getting dirty is apart of the job description of the church planter. Are you willing to get dirty?

Before Noah was a planter, he was a builder. Before

Noah was a builder, he was a grace seeker. Many times we implement this process backwards. We plant, then build, and then seek the presence of the Lord. The scripture says of Noah,

But Noah found grace in the eyes of the LORD. (Gen. 6:8)

Grace is a powerful concept in the scripture. For the most part, we know grace as unmerited favor, but grace is so much more than forgiveness of sin. Grace is the empowerment of the spirit. Grace is the very presence of God.

> *And I will pour upon the house of David, and upon the inhabitants of Jerusalem, the spirit of grace.. (Zech. 12:10)*

The Spirit of Grace is the Holy Spirit. Noah found more than favor, He found the anointing. The Bible says, in the presence of the Lord, there is the fullness of joy (Psalm 16:11). Notice that it said the fullness of joy. This means there are many different facets to joy. Joy has many different dimensions. Within joy you have peace, happiness, humor, and even strength.

> *...for the joy of the LORD is your strength. (Neh. 8:10)*

In the joy of the Lord there is also a dimension of strength. This is what I believe Noah found. Noah found strength. Why, you ask? I believe that he was going to need supernatural strength to build the ark. Many times church planters launch out to build and plant something magnanimous without understanding the importance of the presence of the Lord. Noah was most importantly, a worshiper. Noah was skilled in building altars and seeking the presence of the Lord. This is why the bible says that Noah "found" grace. Noah was a seeker of the presence of the Lord. Are you a presence seeker? Getting familiar with the presence of the Lord is the first job of the church planter. Understanding the presence is our job and responsibility.

> *These are the generations of Noah: Noah was a*

*just man and perfect in his generations, and Noah
walked with God. (Gen. 6:9)*

Noah was a man of justice. Noah stood for something
other than himself. Noah was a righteousness man, and was
perfect. The word "perfect" means mature. We understand that
Noah was not without fault, he failed quite horribly at times, but
he was a man who had found grace. Since Noah had found
grace, there was no failure that he could not overcome. Now
watch this statement. "And Noah walked with God." Noah had a
personal, intimate, working relationship with the Lord. Noah
walked with God. Every step Noah took, he depended on God
to direct his path. Dependency on God is a great attribute. I
have learned that our walk with God must be nurtured, because
it does not always happen automatically. You have to discipline
yourself to depend on God. Noah was a presence seeker. He
depended on the very presence of the Lord.
Noah was also a builder.

*Make thee an ark of gopher wood; rooms shalt
thou make in the ark, and shalt pitch it within and
without with pitch. And this is the fashion which
thou shalt make it of: The length of the ark shall be
three hundred cubits, the breadth of it fifty cubits,
and the height of it thirty cubits. A window shalt
thou make to the ark, and in a cubit shalt thou
finish it above; and the door of the ark shalt thou
set in the side thereof; with lower, second, and
third stories shalt thou make it.*

*Thus did Noah; according to all that God
commanded him, so did he. (Gen. 6:14-16, 22)*

Noah was obedient. Noah did all that God commanded
him to do. The task before Noah was vast and complex. Noah
had a mission to do something that no man had ever done
before. Have you ever felt like that? It is hard to build something
without an earthly blueprint or model. Moses had this same
problem when building the Tabernacle in the Wilderness. God
has a way of giving us divine blueprints to build divine things.

Do not worry if there is nothing in the earth that resembles what God has shown you, He can show you better than anyone. God specifically laid out the plans for Noah. Noah was never in the dark as it related to God's plan for what he was building. God is meticulous. Not only did God tell Noah what to build, but also God told Noah what to use to build it. God is not a God of the obscure. God is very detailed, even down to the type of wood He wanted Noah to use.

Building was a very important part of Noah's development as a leader. Church planter, you must understand that what God is using you to build, is also building you. Building is a test. This process of building is designed to test Noah's strength, fortitude, courage, obedience, consistency, and stamina. You are being tested. Make no mistake about this, building is supposed to be hard. Building is supposed to be painful. Building is supposed to make you question your calling and your ability. If you are not feeling the pain and anguish of building, chances are what you are building will not have any real value.

> Make thee an ark of gopher wood; rooms shalt thou make in the ark, and shalt pitch it within and without with pitch. And this is the fashion which thou shalt make it of: The length of the ark shall be three hundred cubits, the breadth of it fifty cubits, and the height of it thirty cubits. A window shalt thou make to the ark, and in a cubit shalt thou finish it above; and the door of the ark shalt thou set in the side thereof; with lower, second, and third stories shalt thou make it. (Gen. 6:14-16)

The ark was to have three levels. These levels are very significant to planting a kingdom center. These three levels held the government, structure, and organization of the ark together. Without all three of these levels, the massive ship would have imploded and collapsed. These three levels represent the headship, leadership, and fellowship of the local church. The top level is the headship level. This is the place of vision, which is why the window is placed here. The top level also provides covering and protection from the elements and storms. The second level is the leadership level. This is where all of the wealth is stored and activity takes place. The third level is the fellowship level. This is the foundational level. Where there is no fellowship, the church will not float or have the ability to move. All three levels are needed in order to fulfill its assignment. The largest level is the leadership level, this is the belly of the ship. Let's discover how to build our leadership core in this chapter, *Soldiers and Shoulders*.

Noah was a great man, but even Noah, with all of his grace and might, could not build by himself. You may be reading this, and you may be endowed with intellectual ability. You may be a great preacher and a phenomenal leader, but if you do not have a team of leaders to help you, you will expire prematurely. Teamwork is the key to longevity and sustainable greatness. Jordan, Bryant, and James are legends, graced with incredible skill, but if you forget Pippen, O'Neal, and Wade, you have totally missed the point of greatness. Greatness is developed by who you surround yourself with, not just with the gifts and talents that you possess. What is the purpose of being called to something major, and having no one to share it with? One of the principles that we can extrapolate from the calling of Noah is that when God calls you, He calls you, your family, and your relationships. For this reason alone we must be very cautious and intentional with the relationships that we develop and enter into. I believe that Noah was greatly gifted, but we cannot overlook the importance of his family. Noah was married, and had three sons, who were all married as well. The pattern of marriage that we see in Noah's family reveals to us that relationships were very important to this leader. Teams are all about relationships. Relationships are the currency of the Kingdom of God. The Kingdom of God cannot advance beyond relationships. Our greatest investments will be in the relationships that we have. Developing relationships becomes the first test of your church planting journey. When Jesus first initiated His earthly ministry, the first thing He did was find a team, and begin to develop them. This is your first step.

DEVELOPING LEADERS

Building a core team is one of the hardest, but most important parts of planting a church. Without a solid core, the planter can find himself alone, doing everything by himself. Have you ever felt like you were the only person working? Have you ever felt tired, fatigued, and ready to give up? This could be the result of an inadequate leadership structure. I have found, by speaking with church planters and leaders, that while this is the most important stage, it is also the most neglected. Many church planters skip over this part of the process not knowing that this is where planting begins. Jesus began his ministry, after his baptism and temptation, by finding a suitable team to help him accomplish his assignment. Notice that Jesus did not chooses a team until after he was himself baptized and tempted. These two stages are very significant in the development of a leader, and they become the first signs that someone is ready to be initiated into a higher place of ministry. When choosing leaders, they must first be saved, and then they must be proven.

Not a novice, lest being lifted up with pride he fall into the condemnation of the devil. (1 Tim. 3:6)

Paul is very clear that leaders cannot be novices. Novice is a word that means one who is newly planted, or newly converted. A leader must be clear about the fundamentals of doctrine and history. Our church, Embassy International Worship Center, is a church that focuses on leadership development. We began with the concept that everyone is a leader waiting to be developed. Everything we do is geared towards the leader in a person. I believe that this is a great model to implement. This does not mean that every person that attends your ministry will be a leader in the house, but it does mean that every person who comes is being equipped to lead. Developing leaders takes patience and persistence. Leaders are not only born, but they are grown. We must implement the types of systems, training, and structures that are conducive to developing the quality of leader that will change our communities. When we first started planting in February of

2011, we literally had leadership meetings for months. We did no formal preaching or worship, everything was geared towards leaders. This became an intense time of development and training, because it was needful for where the Lord was taking us. This model is hard to adapt, because most church planters are looking for immediate growth. This step is commonly bypassed because we are looking to gather crowds and not build kingdom centers. Most church planters are guilty of building fan clubs and not true houses of power. One of the ways we begin to address the growing trend of weak churches in America is by focusing on leadership development.

I recommend this as the first step of action. Before you have a name, before you get a building, before you ask anyone to come to your service, gather a group of people that believe in you, and begin developing the leader in them. Notice what I said, I said that they need to believe in you. Those that followed Jesus believed in Him. Now, being a follower of Jesus is definitely a prerequisite, but if your leaders do not believe in you, your church is already doomed to fail. The first thing that people must buy into when they come to your church is you. We try to sell the vision and purpose of the church, all the while the people are looking for a relationship, not to a tagline, but to a person. Developing these relationships are key during the infancy of your planting journey.

How do you get people to buy into you? This is simple; spend time with your people. At this stage of your ministry, it is small enough for you to spend quality time with everyone at the same time. Now this moment must be maximized because it will not last long. Even if your church is small, once you begin to get regular visitors and members, who aren't necessarily leaders, you will not be able to offer this time without seeming discriminatory. It is better to spend consistent, quality time with your people early on in the development of your church. These covenant relationships form the foundation of the fellowship, and become a pattern for others to follow. Building relationships must become a priority to the church planter. Teaching on relationships and demonstrating the power of relationships sets a standard of covenant in our houses that should go beyond the initial leadership. We have to teach our teams how to develop relationships within our churches; it is these relationships that will sustain growth and mature people beyond Sunday morning.

POWER TEAMS

I love watching basketball. I can watch it better than I can play it. In the NBA, there is a current phenomenon called SUPER TEAMS. A Super Team is a team filled with the most talented and successful players. Owners and General Managers will invest mind-blowing amounts of money into getting the right players on their team. No one wants to be average in their field, they want to be champions. Companies, firms, businesses and the like, are now investing major time and finances into their teams. The entire world understands that a shift has occurred. Companies and businesses have moved away from depending heavily on individuals and companies are turning their attention towards teams. Even when it comes to hiring, companies are looking for individuals who have the capacity to work within the confines of teams. Lone rangers are not as valuable anymore. The season for lone rangers has run its course. Lone rangers are great assets, but even worse liabilities. To invest so much time, energy, and money into one person, just for them to expire or leave, is costing companies millions of dollars. There is a reconstruction within the model of production, and this new model is called teams. A team comprises a group of people linked in a common purpose. Teams are especially appropriate for conducting tasks that are high in complexity and have many interdependent subtasks. A group in itself does not necessarily constitute a team. Teams normally have members with complementary skills and generate synergy through a coordinated effort. This allows each member to maximize his or her strengths and minimize his or her weaknesses. Team members must help one another to realize their true potential, and create an environment that allows everyone to go beyond their limitations. The church must understand the importance of building what I call, power teams.

A "Power Team" is a concept that we began to build on when we first started meeting as a group to build Embassy. We, like the NBA, did not want to be average. I believe if you are going to do something, do it the best way the first time around, this eliminates room for regret. "Power" is an adjective that we have developed in the culture of our church. We put the word "power" before many things: power prayer, power preaching, power giving, and of course, power teams. The adjective "power" means the ability to TRANSFORM and to CHANGE. In physics, power is the rate at which work is performed or energy is converted. Power is translated by the equation, work divided by time. Power is determined by how much work can be done over a certain period of time. The more power you have, the less time it takes you to complete an assignment. The less power you have, the more time you need to complete an assignment. Power Teams are highly concentrated groups of leaders, linked together by a common vision to accomplish a common goal. This concept of team ministry is not new. The Bible is replete with examples of teams doing incredible things:

1. Marriages (Adam and Eve)-

Marriages are great examples of power teams. When a man and woman come together in covenant, they form a power source that can transform generations. The family is the first shaper of society, so it has incredible influence and importance. When Adam and Eve were first made, they were made in order. They were made in the image and likeness of God. In Genesis, chapter 3, Adam falls and chaos is released. This lack of order entered and infected every area and sector of society, even the family. So in Genesis, chapter 5, we see something cataclysmic take place.

> *1 This is the book of the generations of Adam. In the day that God created man, in the likeness of God made he him; 2 Male and female created he them; and blessed them, and called their name Adam, in the day when they were created. 3 And Adam lived an hundred and thirty years, and begat a son in his own likeness, after his image...*
> *(Genesis 5:1-3)*

Adam and Eve were created in the image and likeness of God. When Adam fell, him and Eve would begin to produce children, but not after the image and likeness of God. Adam's fall not only affected him, but generations unborn. Adam would produce after his own image and likeness. Human beings would now be limited because of Adam's disobedience. The power source called, the family, is designed to create a nurturing and safe place for the development, correction, and education of the next generation of leaders. This all begins with marriage. This is one of the reasons marriage is under attack in our nation. Family, other than the church, is the only institution ordained by God that has power to change society. Power couples are seen all throughout the Bible, from Adam and Eve, to Abraham and Sarah, Moses and Zipporah, David and Bathsheba, or even Jesus and the Church. Marriage is the foundation of the family, which is the next power team.

2. Families- Noah and his family
3. Saul (Paul) and Barnabas-

Now there were in the church that was at Antioch certain prophets and teachers; as Barnabas, and Simeon that was called Niger, and Lucius of Cyrene, and Manaen, which had been brought up with Herod the tetrarch, and Saul. As they ministered to the Lord, and fasted, the Holy Ghost said, Separate me Barnabas and Saul for the work whereunto I have called them. (Acts 13:1-2)

4. Gideon and 300
5. Joshua and his army
6. Abraham and 318- (Strategic Sons)

And when Abram heard that his brother was taken captive, he armed his trained servants, born in his own house, three hundred and eighteen, and pursued them unto Dan. (Gen. 14:14)

Abraham and the 318

One of the greatest examples of a Power Team is Abraham and the 318. After some godless Kings takes Lot captive, Abraham decides to go and rescue him. Rescuing is an apostolic function. When Jesus came to the Earth, he had power to rescue. Every Kingdom Center, or Apostolic House, has rescuing power. We have the ability to enter regions bound by demonic chains, be it poverty, violence, or perversion, and break the limitations of that city through prayer, evangelism, giving, and preaching. Abraham decides to go after Lot, but he is not going alone, because teamwork makes the dream work. Abraham gets three hundred and eighteen men, born in his own house and pursues them. When it comes to building a team, it is better to raise up gifted individuals within your own ranks, than it is to hire someone outside of your culture. There will be times where we have to hire people who have no invested interested in our ministries for the sake of objectivity, but this is rare. We want to raise up gifts within the house. Abraham did not arm them first. To arm an untrained leader is dangerous. To give a title to a person who does not have the gift, anointing, desire, nor competence to complete the assignment is a recipe for disaster.

The scriptures tell us that these servants were born in Abraham's house. I think this is a key to success for church planters. Not only were these men trained and armed, but they were also servants born within the house. Every church has both servants and sons. It is important to understand the difference. Servants are there primarily for the vision. They serve tenure, and usually after that time, they leave with no attachments. Servants care little about the master; their focus is on the work. Servants are great workers, but can be very hard to form relationships with. A church with nothing but servants can be very cold and legalistic. Church planters, you must develop sons, otherwise your church will be one generational and never fulfill its assignment in the Earth. Sons produce wombs for duplication, and give us the ability to plant our DNA in other cities and nations of the world. Sons are present for the father, and not just the work. Sons want the father's hearts and not just the microphone. Sons should create an atmosphere of impartation and discipline. Sons work hard, not for approval, but from a place of devotion. Sons see the ministry as their own, and take full responsibility for it. Everyone in our churches will not be a son, nor will everyone be a servant, we need both to have balance.

7. Jesus and the Apostles- (Apostolic Teams)

And he called unto him the twelve, and began to send them forth by two and two; and gave them power over unclean spirits; (Mark 6:7)

Sometimes we refer to Power Teams as Apostolic Teams. Apostolic Teams are teams sent on a particular mission, usually to a foreign territory with the purpose of discovery, surveillance, and occupancy. Apostolic Teams usually have the mandate of setting up an embassy. An Apostolic Team is a conglomerate of MEGA GIFTS (highly gifted), trained, equipped, commissioned and SENT OUT to change the spiritual dimension of a region or sector. A Power Team, or Apostolic Team, can be the leadership of a church, the marriage in a family, the board for a business, or legislators of a nation. Apostolic Teams are God's instruments to confront and destroy the demonic kingdom in a given locality. God uses the Apostolic Team to invade the spirit realm of that city and pull down the strongholds and principalities. The spiritual positioning and the anointing which the apostolic team carries gives them a cutting edge in dealing with the spiritual atmosphere over those cities where they are commissioned to go. They are able to POILCE the Heavens and keep them open for the Holy Spirit to be poured out in that city.

Levels of Teams

1. **Association**- are people with different assignments and destiny working on a project. This can be seen in universities, jobs, and churches in a region.

2. **Alliance**- An alliance is an agreement or friendship between two or more parties, made in order to advance common goals and to secure common interests.

3. **Coalition**- a coalition is a pact or treaty among individuals or groups, during which they cooperate in joint action, each in their own self-interest, joining forces together for a common cause.

4. **Covenant**- a binding agreement or alliance in which both parties have responsibilities to fulfill, which bring advancement and blessing.

Power Teams are connected by covenant and not just by contracts. It is important that while you are building your team in the beginning, that money is not a factor. Paying people early is the quickest way to corrupt a relationship. When money is a major factor within the beginning stages of forming your leadership core, you eliminate the ability to mark those that are actually for you and the vision of the church.

> *Now I beseech you, brethren, mark them which cause divisions and offences contrary to the doctrine which ye have learned; and avoid them. (Romans 16:17)*

Paul tells the church at Rome to mark those that cause divisions. The word "mark" is the Greek word *skopeo*, and it is where we get the word "scope" from, which literally means to watch. Paul is admonishing us to watch those, or keep our eye on people that cause divisions. I believe that this is a great principle to apply while building and shaping your core team. Do not just watch those that cause division, but keep a close eye, or watch with scrutiny, those you believe are called to labor with you. Paul tells us to mark them. I think this should be universally applied to all those in leadership. You should mark those who cause division, but mark those who give faithfully, and those who serve without recognition. Mark those who complain, those who are early, and mark the individuals that are chronically late. This level of attention to detail may seem arbitrary at first, but as your church grows and similar personality types begin to emerge, you will understand how invaluable this exercise is. Planting a church is a wonderful process, but working with people can sometimes be underestimated. It is very difficult to lead and coach a team made up of different personalities, preferences, backgrounds, and opinions.

The major stress of leading comes from people, not the

assignment. As your church or organization begins to grow, people with similar personalities will begin to flock towards each other. Personalities seem to have a magnetic pull. They can draw people from miles away without ever having a conversation or initial introduction. Personality pulling can be a great thing, but it can also be a very destructive thing if laws are not in place, especially if you have not marked those among you. As people join the team, and personalities link up, you must be watchful as cliques begin to form. Cliques will destroy a team. It must be clear from the beginning that we are all in this together. Marking becomes very important in the process of building trust. Trust is the glue that keeps your team together and moving forward at a healthy rate. Teams cannot advance further than their level of trust. During leadership meetings, intentionally speak on subjects like honor, trust, and covenant, to build a workable language and expectation among your team. Structuring a workable language and very clear expectations become the foundation for a functional team.

TIMING AND STRATEGY

There are three main attributes that every team must have: Vision, Timing, and Strategy. We will deal with Vision at length in the next chapter, *Bifocals and Seeing Eye Dogs*, but for now let us focus on Timing and Strategy.

> *And of the children of Issachar, which were men that had understanding of the times, to know what Israel ought to do; the heads of them were two hundred; and all their brethren were at their commandment. (1 Chron. 12:32)*

Strategy is knowing what to do, but timing is knowing when to do it. The "when" is the deciding factor in any conquest. Timing is a valuable attribute that cannot be overlooked. A Team is only as good as its timing. My generation has been deemed the "microwave generation." My generation likes everything very fast, with as little effort as possible. Since we live in a celebrity culture, making idols out of one-man shows, we tend to want to do everything ourselves.

This celebrity culture, mixed with our desire to have everything right now, is a dangerous combination. This type of environment breeds selfish leaders, only focused on their anointing and assignment, never truly developing a heart for people. Introverted ministry has become the norm, infecting our preaching and churches, causing outreach to become almost nonexistent. Timing must become a priority among the team, not just the completion of goals, but also the timing of movement.

> And when the cloud was taken up from the tabernacle, then after that the children of Israel journeyed: and in the place where the cloud abode, there the children of Israel pitched their tents (Numbers 9:17)

The scripture tells us that the movement of the children of Israel was based on the movement of the cloud. If the cloud moved, they moved, and if the cloud stayed, they pitched their tent. Timing is extremely important, without it we can find ourselves too early or too late. Being syncopated with the plan of God for your church is vital to the life and success of planting. Every gardener understands that there are seasons more conducive than others. When it comes to timing, we must constantly pray for discernment. Now, I am going to take a very unpopular approach here. Within the church planting world, there has been much research done to find out what are the best times to plant a church. The best times to plant a church, according to many church planting books, are during times of celebrations like Christmas and Easter. I disagree with this. I think the best time to start your church is when the cloud moves. We have made church planting all about gimmicks and statistics, but there is nothing like the voice of the Lord. Leader, you must be significantly sensitive to the voice of the Lord. Your progress is connected to your ability to discern time. Church planter, the worst thing you can do is start your church depending on the statistics of men. There is knowledge available, and there are trends that are helpful to understand how to be productive, but this cannot replace the raw voice of God. When was the last time you asked the Lord the right time to move, or not to move? These types of conversations must be engaged quite frequently.

> *And David enquired at the LORD, saying, Shall I pursue after this troop? Shall I overtake them? And he answered him, Pursue: for thou shalt surely overtake them, and without fail recover all. (1 Sam. 30:8)*

This verse says that David inquired of the Lord. The first thing that David did when he wanted to know whether to pursue or not, David enquired of the Lord. David did not look at the church across the street, or model his movements based on a successful church in the past, these things can be helpful, but first he had a conversation with the Lord. This type of dialogue grows your understanding of timing and demonstrates how to navigate chronologically. Before you begin planting, enquire of the Lord concerning the trajectory of your ministry. When we first began structuring Embassy, the first thing we did was seek the Lord concerning our first 20 years. Before we had one service, we knew where we were going. This produced, not only vision, but also strategy. Timing is the cornerstone of strategy. Without timing, it is hard to know what to do, when to do it, or even what the outcome should look like. The "when" is a big question. This is most likely the question that has halted your progress. When do I start? When do I get a building? When do we move to two services? When do I ordain? When do I hire staff? The "when" is the question that usually determines who will be good, and who will be great. Teams must value timing. Most teams do not work because everyone is moving at their own speed. The job of the leader is to set goals and common objectives, in order to synchronize the steps of the team together. When one person on the team becomes impatient, it becomes a disease that can infect the totality of your church.

> *And the people murmured against Moses, saying, What shall we drink? (Exodus 15:24)*

> *And the whole congregation of the children of*

Israel murmured against Moses and Aaron in the wilderness: (Exodus 16:2)

What began with a few people, eventually matriculated into an entire congregation. You must be watchful for impatience. Patience is a virtue that you must impart into the DNA of your team. Your team must be willing to work longer than the date depicts and go further than the race demands. When impatience enters the camp, murmuring and complaining are sure to follow. Continuing to encourage your team about the importance of timing and constantly setting before them the trajectory of the assignment of the house can rectify impatience. Everything can not be done in the first year, and it is vital that your team understands this. You want people on your team that are with you for the long haul and not for short term success.

Vision is where you are going, but strategy is how you are going to get there. I love the game of chess, and I try to play as often as I can. Chess is a game of strategy. There are those who play chess and there are those who play checkers. Checkers is a game based on reactions. Chess is a game based on responses. Chess develops your ability to recognize and execute moves. Strategy is all about recognizing and executing movements. Timing is knowing the "when," but strategy is knowing the "what." Strategy is defined by dictionary.com as the science or art of combining and employing the means of war in planning and directing large military movements and operations. How a team operates determines their effectiveness, but more importantly, their efficiency. How well does your team work? This is a hard question that leaders must continue to ask. Every time someone joins your team, or leaves your team, it is going to affect the dynamics of your team. Strategy is how your team works together to get things done.

Leaders are made for responsibility. A person that runs away from responsibility is not a leader. Make no mistake about it; you can identify a leader by their response to responsibility. If a person runs toward responsibility, it is usually a sign that a leader is being birthed. If they run away from responsibility, that reveals their inability to handle pressure. Leaders must be able to handle pressure. The purpose of teams is to take some of the burden off of the headship so that they are free to direct and lead. It is almost impossible to lead when leadership never alleviates the burden of responsibility.

13 And it came to pass on the morrow, that Moses sat to judge the people: and the people stood by Moses from the morning unto the evening. 14 And when Moses' father in law saw all that he did to the people, he said, What is this thing that thou doest to the people? why sittest thou thyself alone, and all the people stand by thee from morning unto even? 15 And Moses said unto his father in law, Because the people come unto me to enquire of God: 16 When they have a matter, they come unto me; and I judge between one and another, and I do make them know the statutes of God, and his laws. 17 And Moses' father in law said unto him, The thing that thou doest is not good. 18 Thou wilt surely wear away, both thou, and this people that is with thee: for this thing is too heavy for thee; thou art not able to perform it thyself alone. 19 Hearken now unto my voice, I will give thee counsel, and God shall be with thee: Be thou for the people to God-ward, that thou mayest bring the causes unto God: 20 And thou shalt teach them ordinances and laws, and shalt shew them the way wherein they must walk, and the work that they must do. 21 Moreover thou shalt provide out of all the people able men, such as fear God, men of truth, hating covetousness; and place such over them, to be rulers of thousands, and rulers of hundreds, rulers of fifties, and rulers of tens: 22 And let them judge the people at all seasons: and it shall be, that every great matter they shall bring unto thee, but every small matter they shall judge: so shall it be easier for thyself, and they shall bear the burden with thee. (Exodus 18:13-22)

This is an amazing passage. Moses was an exceptional

leader. He was a renaissance man, who could almost everything, but the toll responsibility was taking on Moses could not be hidden from Jethro, his father-in-law. Jethro acted as a spiritual father to Moses, but I believe his role as a coach in Moses' life, helped him deal with the pressure of leadership. Coaches are needed within the spheres of teams. You father your children, you pastor your congregation, but you must coach your team. Coaching is a necessary dimension of pastoring that must be cultivated and enhanced if your team is going to be successful. All throughout Moses' administration, you see Jethro at key moments like this one, not to dictate Moses' decisions, but to fine tune his steps. This is what a coach does. A coach sees every moment as an opportunity to develop the team and its members. A coach lightly corrects and modifies in order to bring about a greater level of accuracy and effectiveness. Do you remember when Moses' gift was first recognized? Moses was born to be a leader, but he did not understand his gift. When Moses saw someone in trouble, his first inclination was to kill them. He was gifted, but without oversight, his gift killed people. This is why teams are important. You may have many gifted people within your house, but without a great coach, their gift could potentially kill people in the congregation. Jethro was Moses' coach, and through him, Moses became a skilled leader. In the passage above, we see Moses spending all of his time judging the cases of Israel. I love what Jethro says in verse 17, he tells Moses, "This is not good." As a coach, your job is to identify the weaknesses of your team and address them head on. You can not build a power team if you are afraid to address the weaknesses. Addressing weaknesses in any structure must be coupled with the ability to empower and encourage as well.

A false balance is abomination to the LORD: but a just weight is his delight. (Prov. 11:1)

As a coach, you must find the balance between correction and construction, too much of any one will cause an imbalance. After Jethro identifies this potentially assignment-assassinating habit, he gives Moses a suggestion.

21 Moreover thou shalt provide out of all the people able men, such as fear God, men of truth, hating covetousness; and place such over them, to be rulers of thousands, and rulers of hundreds, rulers of fifties, and rulers of tens: 22 And let them judge the people at all seasons: and it shall be, that every great matter they shall bring unto thee, but every small matter they shall judge: so shall it be easier for thyself, and they shall bear the burden with thee. (Exodus 18:21-22)

Jethro tells Moses to choose a leader from among the people in order to help alleviate some of the pressure. Notice that Jethro tells Moses to choose "able men." Able men are people with ability. When choosing those that will make up your power team, choose able men. Choose people who have the capability to accomplish the task ahead and not just the people available for the moment. You can save yourself so many headaches by not appointing people according to the need of the moment, but according to the direction of the vision. Choose people who are able and willing to serve, and not just those who have the credentials. Jethro says to choose men that fear God; this means they have a relationship with the Holy One. Jethro says, choose men of truth, which are honest and upright men. Jethro says, choose men that are content with their own possessions and gifts. Why do you not want covetous people on your team? People who are jealous of others tend to compete with others. The last thing you want on your leadership team is competition. Every individual on a team must be fully content and aware of their own gifting and calling. Every leader won't have the same capability, but they can flourish in their assignment. When a person steps outside of their place of appointment, they cannot help but become a disappointment. Moses was to choose men that had the capacity to manage and to judge, some thousands, some hundreds, some fifties, and some ten. Each man had the same qualifications, but not the same capacity. Qualifications level the playing field, not responsibility. This must be understood within the context of a team so that comparison does not cause division. We may not have the same job, but we were chosen based on the same qualifications.

> 14 For the kingdom of heaven is as a man traveling into a far country, who called his own servants, and delivered unto them his goods. 15 And unto one he gave five talents, to another two, and to another one; to every man according to his several ability; and straightway took his journey. (Matthew 25:14-15)

The man called his servants and gave each one of them talents according their "several ability" or their capacity. He gave one man five, one two, and the other one, he wasn't trying to be fair, but he was being just. We can not give everyone the same responsibility and weight, but everyone can do something. Jethro understood this and so he tells Moses to choose men who can handle different measures. One of the jobs of the coach is to discern the capacity of the team members. Discerning a leader's capacity can be a frustrating process. This process is usually done through trial and error. You can not be afraid of giving leaders responsibility, even when you know that there is a possibility of failure. Failure is something that you must see as a fundamental stage of growth. There will be failure. Let me repeat this, THERE WILL BE FAILURE! The sooner your team understands failure's purpose, the quicker you can bounce back from defeats. Teams do not have to time to allow failure to weaken their morale and limit their drive.

Jethro says that the purpose of forming this leadership structure is so that the burden will be taken off of Moses. This is the main function of a team, especially your leadership, to alleviate the pressure and burden from the headship. Moses had tremendous weight resting on him because of his assignment, and he needed help. Many times building leadership is overlooked because of pride. Most leaders hate to admit they need help. Leaders see asking for help as a sign of weakness, but it is actually a sign of strength. The ability to admit that you don't know everything takes gallons of confidence and security. Building teams is to help you, not hurt you. In Exodus, chapter 17, Moses needed help. As Joshua, his son in the faith, fought the Amalekites in the valley, Moses went to the mountain top to worship. It was impossible for Moses to do this alone. Moses as a human being was finite. So what did Moses do? He took with him Aaron and Hur.

> 11 And it came to pass, when Moses held up his hand, that Israel prevailed: and when he let down his hand, Amalek prevailed. 12 But Moses' hands were heavy; and they took a stone, and put it under him, and he sat thereon; and Aaron and Hur stayed up his hands, the one on the one side, and the other on the other side; and his hands were steady until the going down of the sun. (Exodus 17:11-12)

When Moses worshipped, Israel won. When Moses' hands got heavy and began to drop, Israel faced difficulty. There is a great principle found in this. Church planter, leader, and pastor, your degree of worship is directly connected to your team's success. Worship not only provides an elevated view to oversee the affairs of your house, but it also strengthens those who are under you to win their battles. Exodus tells us that Aaron stood on one side, and Hur stood on the other, placing a rock under Moses. The rock under Moses is Christ. Christ must be our foundation. Our team can hold up our hands, but they cannot hold up our lives. As planters, we have to have a healthy level of expectation towards our teams. We cannot expect our teams to do something that only Christ can do. Aaron represents intercession, and Hur's name actually means nobility, which speaks of honor. Two irreplaceable attributes, that must be present within your team, are intercession and honor. If they can not pray with you, they can not lead with you. Honor is a culture that must be grown strategically; we will deal with this in depth in the chapter, *Greenhouses and Habitats*.

BUILDING YOUR TEAM

When we speak about developing power teams, we are dealing with the gathering of key individuals with Character, Competence and Chemistry. These individuals can produce results within a set period of time. Make no mistake about it, teams must produce results. Teams must be gathered around vision. They must move together according to correct timing and utilize the same strategy in order to accomplish their goals. I want to introduce a concept I call, the 3 C's. The 3 C's is what I look for when choosing potential leaders and those that will serve around me. While Moses chose able men to deal with small judgements, he called Aaron and Hur to walk closer to him. This brings me to the subject of leadership levels. Within a given house there will be levels of leadership teams. Our house, Embassy International, has a four level leadership structure: headship, which is the set man and his family, the Executive Team, which is made up of those closest to the set man, and then we have our power team and the fellowship, which is the main congregation. Jesus demonstrated this within His own ministry. Jesus had the seventy, which he sent out two by two. Jesus had the twelve and he also had the three, which consisted of Peter, James, and John. It is impossible to have the same level of relationship with everyone on your team, and this must be made abundantly clear to erase any chance of jealousy or discrimination.

Church planter, hear me clearly; you have the right to choose those who surround you. Be as meticulous as possible choosing those who will be close to you. You want to find people you are comfortable, compatible, and cohesive with. Church planter, you can never apologize about this. People will make you feel guilty that you are not giving them equal attention, but this is not your job. If you gave everyone equal attention, you would have no time to do what God has called you to do. Leaders must be there for you, but not because of you. There is a big difference. When choosing your team, the 3 C's become the standard by which you choose your teammates. Are you ready to choose your team?

Everyone that you choose must be strategic. Notice that I said, "choose." It is important to encourage the entire congregation to volunteer their service and time for the building of the ministry, but when it comes to leadership, that is an invited place. Leaders that force and manipulate their way into leadership will divide a house, but those invited should operate in humility, knowing that it is a place of delegated authority. The

3 C's is the criteria that I suggest church planters use as a basis for structuring a team. Character, Competence and Chemistry are so vitally important that no team can survive without them.

Character

Leaders must be people of character. When building a team, character can not be skipped. Every team member must be upright and just. Character can be camouflaged, so this takes time. When choosing leaders, take your time. Rushing to put leaders in a position can destroy your ministry before it is ever launched. There are several ways that character is produced and checked.

Anonymity - Not giving people titles at the beginning can save you a lot of trouble. People are naturally territorial. The giving of titles makes this even worse. Assigning people specific duties and responsibilities is encouraged, but do this without giving anyone a title. There should be a period of time that a partner has to serve before they are considered for leadership. At Embassy International, a partner must have clocked 30 hours of volunteer time before they are even considered for leadership. Not giving people titles is a sure way to weed out those who are only looking for authority and don't truly posses a heart for service.

Accountability- There is no way for a leader to hold his entire congregation accountable directly, but he can hold his team accountable. Evaluations become a key to determining a leaders attitude and location of maturity. Character can be overshadowed by service during the process of planting a church. It is easy to mistake someone who works hard, with someone who is hard working. Just because someone is proficient, does not mean that they are pure. Evaluations can be done creatively or organically. We have done everything from comment cards, leadership interviews, to dinner. Do not neglect the power of one on one conversation as it relates to determining a person's character. It is not much a person can hide when you are face to face. Keeping someone accountable helps them understand that you are here for them, and conditions them to submit to your counsel, being open and honest about their struggles.

Attendance- Why choose a leader who is never there? Attendance is critical when it comes to positioning leaders. A leader can not be effective if they are not present. I would suggest, at the beginning of structuring your leadership core, take attendance and remind your team how important it is to be present and punctual. Punctuality is just as significant as attendance. Leaders set the tone for the congregation, and if they are constantly late, you can bet that people will be late also. One of the things that reduces a leader's value is when a leader uses excuses. The inability of a leader to admit when they are wrong is detrimental to their character. With some leaders it is always the proverbial "something." Some leaders have more drama than primetime television, and this must be addressed. You must demand a leader's presence. Our leaders know that if we have any event, they need to be there. The presence of leaders validates the event and brings stability to the house.

Character is invaluable, and cannot be replaced. We must constantly check the character of our leaders. Paul writes to Timothy as he is getting ready to choose leaders, and this is what Paul says,

> *2 A bishop then must be blameless, the husband of one wife, vigilant, sober, of good behaviour, given to hospitality, apt to teach; 3 Not given to wine, no striker, not greedy of filthy lucre; but patient, not a brawler, not covetous; 4 One that ruleth well his own house, having his children in subjection with all gravity; 5 (For if a man know not how to rule his own house, how shall he take care of the church of God?) 6 Not a novice, lest being lifted up with pride he fall into the condemnation of the devil. (1 Tim. 3:2-6)*

The word "bishop" here literally means anyone who has

oversight over another, and mirrors the ministry of an elder in the New Testament church. Paul addresses everything from the sexuality of the leader, to the social life of the leader, both are equally important. Paul lists here major attributes to choosing a leader. Character must be the sole attribute that is sought after, after Character everything else will follow.

Competence

There are some great people in our churches, but just because they are great people does not mean they can get the job done. Everyone on your team must have the ability to do the job, or you will be extremely disappointed. Gift must be coupled with skill in order to accomplish an assignment. One thing about competence is that it is never complete because technology is always growing. When it comes to competence you must continually address the element of education by offering classes and encouraging reading, and investing in workshops and conferences. A leader that does not invest in their own development does not deserve your investment into their development. Competence is about skill, and skill must always increase according to the need of the season. We must ask the question, when choosing leaders, can they get the job done? Giving leaders assignments that are time sensitive can test competence. Again, you can not be afraid to use failure as the backdrop to a greater lesson. Sometimes I will give a leader an assignment that I know is too big for them, just to stretch them. Leaders must be occasionally stretched. Leaders must be, and will be tested. Start off by giving leaders small assignments and gradually increase their level of responsibility. Giving a leader too much, too quickly, can break them mentally, physically, and emotionally.

Competence is determined by a number of factors. We can not always see a lack of competence as an indication on one's skill or training. Sometimes a lack of competence is just the result of stress or poor health. Sometimes a lack of competence is the result of the work environment, not necessarily the gift itself. This is why, while planting you must offer your leaders a chance to grow, by focusing on leadership in a unique way. Leaders need special attention and specialized training. We created an avenue to consistently grow our leaders through L.E.A.D. meetings. L.E.A.D. stands for Leaders Engaging in Advanced Development. Churches around the world have adopted this model now. L.E.A.D. meetings are times of empowerment just for our core leaders and volunteers. During these times of sharing we are very transparent and direct. I believe that these times are the most important, and in these times God takes the spirit that is upon you, and places it on your leaders.

> *And the LORD came down in a cloud, and spake unto him, and took of the spirit that was upon him, and gave it unto the seventy elders: and it came to pass, that, when the spirit rested upon them, they prophesied, and did not cease. (Numbers 11:25)*

Moses again found himself in a place of need, and the Lord God spoke to Moses and told Moses to form yet another leadership structure. Now Moses has Aaron, Hur and Miriam, he has the captains that preside over the thousands, hundreds, fifties and tens, and now he has the seventy. The seventy are going to be unique because they are going to carry the spirit of Moses. Teams must carry the spirit of their leader. Moses didn't need workers, he needed leaders. Leaders are not only those that can complete assignments, but those who can carry the opinion and nature of their leader into every situation. This is not to suggest that leaders do not have a mind of their own, but to be able to think like your leader is an invaluable asset. The team must become an extension of the leader's jurisdiction and gift. The team enables the leader to be in more than one place at any given moment. Moses needed someone who would think like him, operate like him, and speak like him, and this is what happened when they became carriers of what was on Moses' life. The scripture says that when Moses' spirit rested upon them, they began to prophesy. Now up until this point, Moses was the only one that prophesied. Moses was known as a prophet and communicated as such. The reason that this is such a heavy statement is because this event marked the beginning of a new era. Team ministry was taking on a new shape. At this moment, leadership was not about assignments, but about relationship. There is something that connects us beyond work, we now have covenant. We are carrying the same assignment. This is the purpose and mission of a team. This type of ministry is only produced when quality time is spent between the leader and his team. This must be a priority to the church planter. I can not stress this enough. If your team is going to be competent, they must have your spirit, and this can be identified when they begin to speak like you. How much time do you spend with your team?

Chemistry

In all of my research about church planting and leadership development, I seldom hear people speak on the subject of chemistry. You can have leaders of great character and skill, but if they do not work well with the other team members, they can become divisive and counter productive. I have found that most teams are not able to accomplish very small tasks because of a few people that refuse to work together. A team is not the place for lone rangers or ball hogs. If a person can not work well with others, they can never expect to be effective in the Kingdom of God. Remember, the Kingdom of God is all about relationships.

Chemistry deals with the interaction of ones personality with another. You can not discount the power of personality when it comes to building your team. Personality is just as important as competence and character. Chemistry deals with how a leader mixes with other leaders. A leader's attitude, perspective, and maturity make up their composition. Each leader is unique and must be strategically placed within your leadership structure. Team members must add to the team and not subtract. One of the main components of chemistry is reaction. Reactions occur when two personalities confront one another. Crisis management should be in place whenever people are gathered together. Wherever there are people, there will be a crisis. Chemistry allows us to track the crisis, and predict when and where they will occur. By understanding the personality and disposition of those who make up your team, you can successfully manage moments of intense pressure.

And we beseech you, brethren, to know them which labour among you, and are over you in the Lord, and admonish you; (1 Thess. 5:12)

Paul admonishes us to know those who labor among us. The word "know" here is the Greek word *eido*, which means to see, discern, to discover or pay attention. Church planters can not be so distracted with the issue of planting, that they forget to pay attention to those who labor among them. Knowing whom you work with gives you wisdom and contributes to the success of the team. We understand our missions and assignments, but without understanding our teammates, offense is sure to come. Offense must be guarded against. When formulating your team, there will be problems, but teams must learn to disagree without causing division. Offense comes to cause division. There is no possible way offense can reside together with unity. Offense is a cancer that comes to kill teams and ministries. There is nothing that kills chemistry like offense.

Now what is offense? Offense is something that offends or displeases someone. It is a violation or the breaking of a law. To "take offense" means to feel humiliated, injured, or annoyed. Wherever there are people, there will be offense. This is why it agitates me when I hear people say they left a church, or "the church," because of offense. No matter how many times you were offended at work, you never left. As many times as family has offended you, you still went to the cook out and the reunions. As many times as you could have been offended at a restaurant or a theater, that doesn't make you stop eating or going to the movies. The reality is people will find anything to make a catalyst for offense.

Offense breeds defensive people. Defensive people are people who feel it is necessary to always be one step ahead of you. These are people who, if they think you are going to break up with them, they will break up with you first just to avoid embarrassment. Defensive people are usually chronic liars and vivid imaginators. They dwell in suspicion and have a false sense of persecution. They think everyone is after them. Sustained unity is one of the keys to growth in any organization. A healthy atmosphere and culture is needed for anything to be successful and impacting. One of the main deterrents to a healthy culture is offense.

> *A brother offended is harder to be won than a strong city: and their contentions are like the bars of a castle. (Prov. 18:19)*

"A brother offended" gives us insight into how offense travels. Offense can only exist where there is relationship. Offense does not occur where there is not expectation. David said in Psalm 55:12-14:

> *12 For it was not an enemy that reproached me; then I could have borne it: neither was it he that hated me that did magnify himself against me; then I would have hid myself from him: 13 But it was thou, a man mine equal, my guide, and mine acquaintance. 14 We took sweet counsel together, and walked unto the house of God in company.*

It wasn't a stranger that offended David; it was someone that he was close to. Offense only happens within the confines of covenant. The scripture says, "A brother offended is harder to win than a strong city." A strong city or stronghold is designed to keep people out and hold things in. It is characterized by its defenses. It gains strength by division. Offense will always cause division. People who are offended separate themselves and become reclusive.

Another result of offense is the spirit of murder. The spirit of murder, hate, and infirmity follows those who are constantly offended.

And then shall many be offended, and shall betray one another, and shall hate one another. (Matthew 24:10)

Do you see the process? Offense breeds betrayal, betrayal breeds hate, hate is the foundation for murder. When we look at the story of Cain and Abel (Gen. 4:1-14), we see this process clearly. Cain became offended with his brother Abel because he received respect from God, and Cain didn't. Cain also was offended with God. I want to point out here that neither God nor Abel did anything wrong, but offense was still present. Offense is not always the result of wrongdoing, but is usually the result of misunderstanding.

> *13 And Cain said unto the LORD, My punishment is greater than I can bear. 14 Behold, thou hast driven me out this day from the face of the earth; and from thy face shall I be hid; and I shall be a fugitive and a vagabond in the earth; and it shall come to pass, that every one that findeth me shall slay me. (Gen. 4:13-14)*

Offense not only caused Cain to kill his brother, but also caused Cain to run from the presence of the Lord. It also says that he became a vagabond, which is a wondering man without any place to dwell. An inability to worship, serve, submit, and be planted in a local church, is all signs of offense. We must understand the responsibility of the "offended" and not just the "offender" to restore order and unity.

Bifocals
and
Seeing Eye Dogs

Chapter Four

Developing a Vision

And he spake a parable unto them, Can the blind lead the blind? Shall they not both fall into the ditch? (Luke 6:39)

A ministry without vision is like a man without sight. A man may be strong, intellectual, and even wise, but without his sight he is crippled and decelerated tremendously. Ministries without vision are dramatically disadvantaged. Most ministries know this, and this is why churches, and companies alike, to develop a vision and mission for their respective brands, spend millions of dollars. Developing a vision for most churches boils down to hashing out neat tag-lines. Developing a vision for your ministry is more than cute phrases and marketing words used to attract people. If the language you use to describe your church is lacking in substance from the actual experience, people will feel cheated and used. Vision is the blood of the ministry. Vision gives the ministry life, power, and direction. Vision acts as a guideline to filter activities that could be superfluous and be energy drainers. Vision is so important to the life of a ministry, without it people work without understanding the "why" of what they do. Churches can experience burn out before they breakthrough any major barriers because of a lack of vision. Everything done in an organization without the presence of vision can seem futile and cause immense fatigue. Vision acts as the glue that holds a team together. A group of people that may not have chemistry can still achieve great results when they have a common vision. Without vision, teams have no lasting bond.

Where there is no vision, the people perish: but he that keepeth the law, happy is he. (Proverbs 29:18 KJV)

If people can't see what God is doing, they stumble all over themselves; But when they attend to what he reveals, they are most blessed. (Message)

Without a Vision is a people made naked, And whoso is keeping the law, O his happiness! (Young's Literal)

When prophecy shall fail, the people shall be scattered abroad: but he that keepeth the law, is blessed. (Douay-Rheims)

Without prophetic vision people run wild, but blessed are those who follow [God's] teachings. (God's Word Translation)

Vision is power. I love looking at different translations and noticing the different word choices they use to describe something seemingly understood. The purpose of a vision has become so diluted, that it has no power in the American church. The first century church was driven by pushed by the vision they received from Jesus, the Messiah. From these scriptures we see that vision is so much more then just a nice synopsis of what your church is about. Vision is the cement that gives your ministry a highway to drive on. The scriptures show us that vision is prophetic. Vision is the prophetic picture of your future that gives you force to outlive your present, and break free from your past. Vision is the fuel of your church. Periodically your church will begin to slow down and stagnate, this is a sign that it is time to reiterate the vision. Vision is supernatural. It is God who gives vision. Vision should not be the result of wishful thinking or ambition, it must be God ordained. Church planters, the worst mistake you can make is to create your own vision. God is not obligated to fund our vision, but He is bound to make His vision come to pass. When God gives us a picture of our future, we can then move with confidence, understanding that what He started, He will complete.

Being confident of this very thing, that he which hath begun a good work in you will perform it until the day of Jesus Christ: (Phil. 1:6)

And Jehovah saith unto me, `Thou hast well seen: for I am watching over My word to do it.' (Jer. 1:12 Young's Literal)*

When God gives you a promise, He watches over that promise to protect and perform it. The Young's Literal Translation says that God is watching over His word to "do" it. God wants to do something great with you, but it all begins with vision. God begins all vision with a promise. We see this principle in the life of Abraham.

And he brought him forth abroad, and said, Look now toward heaven, and tell the stars, if thou be able to number them: and he said unto him, So shall thy seed be. (Gen. 15:5)

In Genesis, chapter 12, Abraham is given a promise. God tells Abraham to forsake all, much like Jesus asked his disciples when he said, "follow me." God promises Abraham that if he would go to a special "place" then he would bless him. In Genesis 15:5, God reminds Abraham of the promise, but this time God puts a picture with the promise, this is called vision. Vision is a picture of the promise. The powerful thing about this experience with Abraham is that there was nowhere Abraham could go to get away from the stars. Every night, when the sun would go down, Abraham was reminded of the promise of God over his life. God kept the vision always before Abraham in order to keep him focused on his goal. A house without vision is a house without focus. It is hard to focus without vision. Vision gives us a clear picture to focus on. This is why the scripture says without vision, people cast off all restraint. There is nothing that holds people together when there is no vision. Many churches today replace vision with programs or events. A church can not become an agent of transformation without a vision. Churches will often substitute vision with movement.

Moving without vision is like a train without tracks. Movement does not equal productivity, and that is all you have when there is no vision in a house. Local churches must understand the importance of vision. Without vision people run wild.

I WANT TO SEE

A life without vision is a meaningless life. Martin Luther King said that a person who won't die for something is not fit to live. Vision becomes the very purpose of our existence, without it we have no reason to live. God gave Adam a vision in the very beginning.

> *And God blessed them, and God said unto them, Be fruitful, and multiply, and replenish the earth, and subdue it: and have dominion over the fish of the sea, and over the fowl of the air, and over every living thing that moveth upon the earth. (Gen. 1:28)*

God gave Adam a simple, concise, but very weighty assignment. The vision of Adam was to establish dominion, or the rule and authority of God in the Earth, through the technology of being fruitful, multiplying, replenishing, subduing and only then could the vision be fulfilled. Not only did Adam have a vision, but with the vision came also directions from God. A vision is the prophetic destination of a ministry. Without understanding the vision, there will always be a lack of direction. Have you ever tried to get somewhere without a map? We live in an age where GPS and satellite navigations are one button away. My city, Atlanta, is a big city, and while navigation is helpful, nothing beats the navigational expertise of a native. Natives can tell you, not just where you are going, how to get there, but pitfalls along the way. Natives can tell you the roads to take, and even side streets that no one has ever heard of. This is why we must spend time in the presence of the Lord, allowing him to give us the vision for our house. Cookie cutter visions lack power, and the personal conviction needed to build in the midst of famine and barrenness. Emerging leaders must have vision. Many church planting networks make barren the womb of the next generation, feeding them clichés and catch phrases that carry no prophetic weight. The cry of our leaders must be "I WANT VISION!!!!"

> *And they came to Jericho: and as he went out of Jericho with his disciples and a great number of people, blind Bartimaeus, the son of Timaeus, sat by the highway side begging. (Mark 10:46)*

When there is no vision, churches become beggars. Churches beg for money, members, influence, and power. A lack of vision breeds poverty. Bartimaeus was a beggar. He had no substance or sight, but he had faith. Bartimaeus understood the importance of visitations. When Jesus was passing by, he saw it as an opportune time to get something that he desperately needed, not money, but his sight. A church with vision can do things that others churches can't do. A church with vision can inspire a community, a city or a nation. A church with a vision can become a catalyst for reformation and revival no matter where it is planted. Bartimaeus knew that if he had asked for money, his lack of vision would have caused him to return to the same place in a season, but vision gave him the power to get wealth.

> *But thou shalt remember the LORD thy God: for it is he that giveth thee power to get wealth, that he may establish his covenant which he sware unto thy fathers, as it is this day. (Deut. 8:18)*

I believe the power to get wealth is vision. There is nothing that can destroy a person, ministry, anointing or gift like having money without vision. Money without vision can destroy a ministry quicker than sin or division. Someone yell "I WANT TO SEE." This must be the cry of our heart. Lord, give us vision to see the unseeable. Declare this with me aloud:

I have perfect vision. My eyes can see the impossible. Father, give me vision for families, city, and nations. Like Abraham, show me a picture of the future supernaturally and give me the courage to step out in faith to see it come to pass. Father we break the curse of blindness and barrenness, and we declare that the famine of vision is over. I am a man/woman of vision. I have a family of vision. We are a church of vision. In Jesus' name, Amen.

VISIONARIES

If you are reading this book, you are undoubtedly a visionary. You are called to an incredible task. Visionaries are phenomenal people. Visionaries choose to look beyond the now and live in the future. Visionaries are timeless beings, always frustrated with the limitations of the present. Nothing moves fast enough for visionaries. Visionaries must learn to balance their insatiable hunger for success with the wisdom of strategy. Strategy places a timetable within the confines of our timelessness and brings balance to our vision. Visionaries have learned to live in two places at once, the present and the future. Visionaries lead a very stressful life. Like Moses, leading people to a place and not actually knowing how to get there is difficult. Every church planter, pastor and leader would love to tell those that follow them, "hey, I know everything. I know where we are going, and exactly how we are going to get there." This couldn't be any further from the truth.

Now the LORD had said unto Abram, Get thee out of thy country, and from thy kindred, and from thy father's house, unto a land that I will shew thee: (Gen. 12:1)

God told Abraham, to get out of his country, away from his family, and his father's house, and go to a land that God would show him. Notice that God never told Abraham where he was going; God just said, "I've got something I want you to see." Godly vision has the power to pull you out of your present circumstance and into a future you could only dream of. Godly vision has the force of magnetism, and it will pull everything and everyone, who is called to stand with you, right by your side. Don't you dare underestimate the power of vision. God is saying, "I want to show you something that you've never seen before. I want to take you on a journey you've never imagined. I want to make your dreams come true, but you have to step out of the boat. If you step out, I will step in, and we can change the world together." Visionaries have ridiculous faith.

> *4 Now there are diversities of gifts, but the same Spirit. 5 And there are differences of administrations, but the same Lord. 6 And there are diversities of operations, but it is the same God which worketh all in all. 7 But the manifestation of the Spirit is given to every man to profit withal . 8 For to one is given by the Spirit the word of wisdom ; to another the word of knowledge by the same Spirit; 9 To another faith...*
> *(1 Cor. 12:4-9)*

Almost everyday I pray for, and ask God to strengthen the Gift of Faith in my life. Paul, teaching the church at Corinth about the working of Holy Spirit, says that there is a gift called faith. This gift of faith is the God type of faith.

And Jesus answering, saith to them: Have the faith of God. (Mark 11:22 Douay-Rheims)

The gift of faith is not natural faith, nor is it intellectual confidence. The gift of faith is literally the faith of God. Visionaries need the gift of faith to move mountains and walk on water. You have been called to be a mountain mover. You have been called to be a water walker. If you have been called to move mountains and walk on water, then understand nothing is going to be easy. Trials and hardships are a visionary's best friend. Visionaries thrive in hard places. If you are in a hard place, pray for the gift of faith. Visionaries live to break records and statistics, creating new pathways for others to follow. Can we pray again? Put your hand on your head, and pray this prayer aloud, with faith and power:

I am a visionary. My calling demands faith. Father, I ask now for supernatural faith. Not the faith of men, but the faith of God. Father, give me your faith. Give me the strength and bravery to run through troops, and leap over walls. Give me faith that transcends nationality, financial bracket, church size or notoriety. Lord, give me faith that shakes the city.

Visionaries have the responsibility to make sure everyone around them is equipped with the vision. This can be a challenging thing. Personal vision is easy, but translating personal vision into corporate responsibility can be mind-boggling. There are 3 stages of impartation when it comes to vision. Vision cannot solely be taught, it must be grabbed spiritually. If our houses are going to grow in a healthy way, the vision of the ministry must be grabbed, and carried by every member of the house. When members grab hold of the vision and take personal responsibility for it, they shift from members to partners. At Embassy International, we do not call our congregation members; we call them partners, which implies that they have responsibility. Remember, we want to build a culture of leaders. This doesn't mean your congregation will not understand how to follow, because the best leaders were at some point the best followers. Raising a house of leaders ensures that legacy is built and generations are touched beyond you. The job of the visionary is to impart the vision to the house. The three stages of imparting vision is:

1. Inspiration
2. Information
3. Inundation

Before we get into the meat of this, let us deal very basically with the technology of impartation. The word "technology" is being used to define a grace or tool used to get a job done. Impartation is a supernatural technology that we as Believers have. By faith we have the ability to share gifts, heal, and even set and ordain elders in the Lord's church. God puts tremendous power in our hands.

For I long to see you, that I may impart unto you some spiritual gift, to the end ye may be established; (Romans 1:11)

The word "impart" here is the Greek word *metadidomi*, which is made up of two Greek words. The first Greek word is *meta*, where we get words like metaphysics and metamorphic.

The Greek word *meta* literally means change. The second Greek word that makes up the word "impart" is the word *didomi*, and it literally means to give. Impartation is when one is changed by what is given to them. When you receive impartation, your life is changed forever. Giving someone something is not impartation. Giving someone something that changes their value is impartation. To impart means to give, share, or release a portion of something supernaturally. Impartation is the grace that strategically releases specialized degrees and facets of the anointing into another person's life, for the purpose of Kingdom advancement.

Neglect not the gift that is in thee, which was given thee by prophecy, with the laying on of the hands of the presbytery. (1 Tim. 4:14)

Paul told his spiritual son Timothy, do not neglect what has been given to you by impartation. That word "give" in this scripture is the word *didomi* again. Paul shared something with Timothy that was supernatural. If we are going to see the power shift from servants to sons, we need an impartation of vision. Vision must be imparted.

Inspiration

All vision begins with inspiration. Vision comes first to inspire, then to perspire. Excitement without work changes nothing. Excitement is the first stage of vision impartation. Quite frankly, people have to become excited about what God desires to do in your church and city. Now this is the part you have to listen to. Getting people excited about the vision is not God's job, that is your job. Church planter, you have to find creative ways to get your church and community excited about the vision that God has given you. Inspiration is the first stage of vision, and it is at this stage where everyone will flock to you. The initial stage of the vision is filled with praise and applause. Church planter, you can not become drunk from the first stage of impartation, after excitement comes exposure. One of the ways to get people excited about the vision is to constantly share your story with them, in as many ways as possible. You must create videos, blogs, whatever you can to continue to remind people about your story and your purpose. Excitement must begin with incitement. There is no possible way we can get others excited about a vision we aren't excited about. Excitement and inspiration is contagious, and if you catch it, you can't help but pass it along. In John 4, after Jesus had the conversation with the woman at the well, she left inspired. The Samaritan woman went about her entire city saying, "Come see a man." When people get excited, they can't help but share it with everyone they know. If there is a lack of evangelism in your church, there is probably a lack of excitement, and this is why your church is not growing. Evangelism can be harmful if it is engaged without excitement. As a visionary, you must get people excited.

Information

In order for people to grab the vision, we must make it tangible. This is the difficult part about leadership. How do we make something that is in the future, tangible? This is where vision boards and statements come in handy. Our vision statement is summed up at Embassy International as: Build People, Engage Culture, Impact Nations. If there is nothing else that you know about our church, you will know this. We use these three phrases to dictate and direct everything that we do. If it does not build people, engage culture, or impact the nations of the earth for the Lord Jesus Christ, we are not doing it. Impartation can not be successful without information. If you give someone something, they have to know what you are giving them. We must always keep the vision before the congregation by giving our people as much information as possible. Posting pictures, filling the hallways with banners, constantly sharing the vision through videos, plays, and preaching is a must if the vision is going to be imparted. Vision can not remain ephemeral; it must become solid by establishing it within everything that we do. Vision only grows when it becomes a culture. The vision of the church should be constantly before the congregation. It should be in everything that they see, and everything that they hear. Every January, at our church in Atlanta, we teach on vision. January is what we call our vision month. This is not the only time we deal with vision, but dedicating specific time to focus on the purpose of the ministry is needed. Another way to keep the vision before the eyes of the people is T-shirts, media products and even books. All of these media mediums present a way to inform the people of the vision. All of this creates the third phase of impartation, which is, inundation.

Inundation

Inundation means to flood, cover or overspread with water. Impartation must begin with inspiration. Inspiration attracts and arrests the hearts of men, and makes us understand that the vision is more important than one person or personal opinion. The vision must take precedent and become the fuel of our passion. After inspiration, it's information that now brings clarity and articulation to our emotions, impressions, and expressions. Inspiration touches us, but information teaches us. Inundation becomes the very atmosphere that grows us. Inundation becomes the submergence that we need to drown our fears and doubts. Submergence is needed for power. You can ask Jesus, who understanding and being fully convinced of whom He was, found John the Submerger.

John the Immerser is needed in every ministry that will be effective at imparting the vision. You need people on the team, and in the house, that don't mind being an echo. Vision must fill the house, bouncing off of every wall, within every ministry if we are going to see Godly growth. Ministries die as soon as the vision is lost. What John offered to his age was preparation by saturation. John was consistent, preaching the message of the kingdom, in season and out of season. John saturated Judea with the vision of God for his time. Saturation is important to prepare people for what is coming. As a growing church, you will attract people who are infatuated by where you are now. I remember people coming to me saying, "Pastor I love this church, it is like family. I don't like big churches, I prefer small churches." I would stop people in their tracks, and say, "You should leave now. While we are small now, we do not intend on staying where we are." You have to be intentional about saturating or inundating your church with the vision of the house. How do you do this? Inundation must be a team effort. Inundation must be purposeful and consistent. Every leader on the team must understand their role in presenting the vision before the congregation in a way that inspires and informs. In short, we want to move people from just being members to being vision carriers.

VISION CARRIERS

Vision cannot just be taught; it must be caught, and then carried. When vision is carried, every partner takes a personal responsibility in conveying the vision to the world. The vision of the house is not just meant for the local church, but should be revealed to the community and city to remind them what is on the mind of God for that region. In order for vision to be carried, it must first me casted. Casting vision must go before carrying vision. Casting vision begins with the set man or woman of the house. The vision must be casted first to the leaders. If the transfer of the vision to the leaders is not successful, the house will undoubtedly fall. If the leadership cannot grasp the vision, you can't be confident that the congregation will ever truly come in contact with the vision. There must be times where we test the leadership and the congregation about the contents of the vision.

> *13 When Jesus came into the coasts of Caesarea Philippi, he asked his disciples, saying, Whom do men say that I the Son of man am? 14 And they said, Some say that thou art John the Baptist: some, Elias; and others, Jeremias, or one of the prophets. 15 He saith unto them, But whom say ye that I am? (Matthew 16:13-15)*

Jesus tests his disciples as to the vision or identity of his mission. Jesus engages in market research and finds out that the public didn't really know who He was. Does your city know why you are there? Jesus discovers this by a question. Feedback is one of the greatest ways to determine where the vision is within the process of impartation. Asking people to fill out comments cards or even engaging in casual conversation will be a strong avenue in testing whether people have caught the vision or not. When Jesus asks this question, it is clear that people don't fully understand who He is, so He turns the attention to the disciples. If the congregation does not understand the vision, there must be a disconnection between the people and the leaders. When there is a disconnection between the leadership and the congregation, vision will move very slowly, enthusiasm will ebb, and speed will decrease. Whenever you begin to lose momentum, there is a disconnection in your organization. This is why we, as leaders, must cast vision every chance we get. Vision must be cast during staff meetings, pre-evangelism strategy time, conversations, fellowships, and our main worship gatherings. Church planter, you must take every opportunity to share the vision with your team and those you serve with. Vision drives a team.

Vision must be carried. Vision is heavy. It takes strength to carry vision. Carrying vision can definitely take a toll on anyone. This is why everyone must be a vision carrier. When the Senior Leader is the only person carrying the vision, he or she can feel alone and depressed. If a team is the only force carrying the vision, they can get tired quicker, which will in turn decrease their effectiveness and competence. A church's ability to accomplish its assignment depends on its ability to transfer the vision to everyone. You must be a vision carrier. The modern church produces people who want to be card holders but not vision carriers. The church must shift from membership to partnership. For a long time the majority of the church's work was done by a very small percentage of people, this must change if the church will rise up in power. Casting vision makes everyone responsible to seeing that the vision comes to pass. Vision unifies a church behind a common goal.

ENEMIES TO VISION

Whenever people carry vision, there will be enemies. There are many enemies to vision. Division comes to divide and distort the vision among teams and churches. Doubt, disbelief, fatigue, confusion, and even betrayal become major factors when you are building anything great. Jesus tells a parable about the dangers of building.

> 24 Therefore whosoever heareth these sayings of mine, and doeth them, I will liken him unto a wise man, which built his house upon a rock: 25 And the rain descended, and the floods came, and the winds blew, and beat upon that house; and it fell not: for it was founded upon a rock. 26 And every one that heareth these sayings of mine, and doeth them not, shall be likened unto a foolish man, which built his house upon the sand: 27 And the rain descended, and the floods came, and the winds blew, and beat upon that house; and it fell: and great was the fall of it. 28 And it came to pass, when Jesus had ended these sayings, the people were astonished at his doctrine: 29 For he taught them as one having authority, and not as the scribes. (Matthew 7:24-29)

Church planter you are building something massive and momentous. Anything great will be tested. Jesus, in this parable, deals with building a house. Notice it is not really what is built, but where it is built. One house is built on the sand, and the other is built on the rock. What makes a house? A house is made of many things: the foundation, a roof, windows, doors, and bedrooms. I liken the windows of the house to vision. Every attack Jesus lets us know that will come, affects the vision. Rain blurs the vision. Floods break the vision. Wind distorts the vision. When building anything of significance, you must expect attacks. The enemy, the devil, will attack our people, our churches and our plans. A church that is not equipped to war, is a church already positioned to fail. Vision must be defended. I want to deal with two main enemies to vision, the spirit of Jezebel and the spirit of Judas.

The Spirit of Jezebel

Jezebel is a manipulative spirit, which works within a person for the purpose of subverting and discrediting leadership within a house or era. Jezebel looks to kill the prophetic vision of a church. Vision is vast. There is immediate vision, long term vision, but there is also prophetic vision. Prophetic vision is the ability to see the future of what you are planting or building. Jezebel comes to kill the prophetic in a house.

> *For it was so, when Jezebel cut off the prophets of the LORD.. (1 Kings 18:4)*

Jezebel married King Ahab, who was a weak leader. Jezebel loves to exploit weak and inexperienced leadership. The Spirit of Jezebel is also a spirit of extreme intimidation, and will use the smallest things to accuse you of false and/or faulty leadership. Jezebel is critical. This spirit is always seeking to blame people, and preys on people who are broken, or who have been hurt by the church. Jezebel is always seeking validation so she is always looking for people to join her movement. Jezebel thrives within cliques and gossip gives her strength. This spirit is always looking for power and influence and will hide behind titles, or create a title if one isn't given to her. Jezebel is territorial.

Prophetic vision is important within a house because it charges the people with expectation and faith. Jezebel seeks to kill a church's ability to see into the future by entangling everyone she can with drama. This spirit will stop at nothing to be close to the pastor or leadership, believing that her proximity will give her power and privilege. Jezebel also works to make pastors in a city fight against each other, or desires for leaders to remain isolated by false appearances of competition. This spirit is a master spirit that can rule entire churches or regions. Church planters must be aware of their responsibility to war and watch for the spirit of Jezebel. The scripture says of Jezebel that she worshipped the false gods Baal and Asherah. Notice, she was in Israel, but did not worship the God of Israel. So it is with people bound by Jezebel, they will be in your house, but they will be followers of another vision.

1 Kings 21 records that after Ahab was denied Naboth's vineyard, that he was upset and dismayed. Jezebel saw this emotional fragile state as a moment of opportunity. She began to write letters in the name of the king, because Jezebel will exploit the pastor's authority if they are not careful. This spirit

gains access and control by saying things like "well, the pastor said" or "I know the pastor, they wouldn't agree or like that." Be very careful of people who move in your name or operate in your authority. Every leader or elder will move within the jurisdiction that you give them, they are all under delegated authority, but as soon as they start answering for you without your permission, this is a problem that must be addressed. Most visions are not clear, because leadership is not clear. When people do not know who the final authority is in the house, false authorities will rise up and exploit that weakness. Strong leadership must be established early within the development of a church, or Jezebel will begin to grow. Jezebel guards windows. She hangs around visionaries and vision carriers, looking to be associated with those who have rank. We see this in the fact that when Jehu came to assassinate her, she was hanging around the windows, and was subsequently thrown out of one. Jezebel is attracted to the prophetic. Jezebel hates authentic prophetic ministry. Jezebel is a title lover.

Notwithstanding I have a few things against thee, because thou sufferest that woman Jezebel, which calleth herself a prophetess, to teach and to seduce my servants to commit fornication, and to eat things sacrificed unto idols. (Revelation 2:20)

The scripture says that Jezebel called herself a prophetess. Jezebel is addicted to titles and will manifest and react harshly if people do not "recognize" her anointing and contribution. Unlike Judas, who loves the shadows, Jezebel loves attention. Jezebel will seek to weaken the vision of your church by mixing it with the vision of other churches. Every church has a distinct purpose and mission, mixing it because of competition or suggestion can be devastating. Jezebel always reminds you of what other churches are doing, hoping to incite jealously and comparison. The spirit of Jezebel seeks to portray itself as spiritually concerned with the pastor and direction of the ministry. If you are going to be a house of vision, you will attract Jezebel. One of the ways you can tell if Jezebel is operating in a house is by checking the emotional health of the leadership. Emotional health is just as important as spiritual health when you are building a church. There have been great men and women that were powerful spiritually, but committed suicide, or struggled with substance abuse. Weaknesses within leadership is not always caused by flesh, sometimes it is a demonic assignment carried out through witchcraft and manipulation. When there is tension and drama in a ministry, it drains the pastor of his or her ability to focus, it takes away their strength, and ultimately leaves them physically and emotionally drained. When Elijah was dealing with Jezebel, we see him at this point.

> *1 And Ahab told Jezebel all that Elijah had done, and withal how he had slain all the prophets with the sword. 2 Then Jezebel sent a messenger unto Elijah, saying, So let the gods do to me, and more also, if I make not thy life as the life of one of them by to morrow about this time. 3 And when he saw that, he arose, and went for his life, and came to Beersheba, which belongeth to Judah, and left his servant there. 4 But he himself went a day's journey into the wilderness, and came and sat down under a juniper tree: and he requested for himself that he might die; and said, It is enough; now, O LORD, take away my life; for I am not better than my fathers. (1 Kings 19:1-4)*

Jezebel was after the vision of Israel. Prophets are always on the hit list of Jezebel. If the devil can take away a church's ability to see, it has destroyed that church's effectiveness. Vision is vital, and without it we can not survive. Elijah, running from Jezebel, finds himself hiding and second guessing his assignment. Many of you reading this are in the process of re-launching, or starting over. You have found yourself in a place of doubt, depression, and disbelief, but guess what? It is not over. The way it was with Elijah, so shall it be with you. Elijah was strengthened by bread, which in the scripture usually represents revelation. In order to battle Jezebel, you must move by revelation. It is important when dealing with Jezebelic problems, that you know who you are. Jezebel will always get you to second guess who you are, your decisions, and your movements. "Pastor, are you sure? I don't know pastor, something don't feel right. If it was me," these are some common phrases that enter a ministry through Jezebel. Lower level witchcraft takes place as soulish manipulation through intimidation, control, and super spirituality. Jezebel comes to put out the eyes of vision.

The Spirit of Judas

The second major force that comes to steal and kill vision within a local church is the spirit of Judas. The Spirit of Judas is the spirit of betrayal. Whenever you work with people you run the risk of betrayal. Regardless of how long you have been in ministry, whether you are pastoring a small church or a big church, betrayal is inevitable. Church planter get ready, you may not want to think about it, but if it has not happened yet, get ready because you are going to be betrayed. Betrayal is like a rite of passage for great people. True betrayal can not occur by those outside of your sphere of influence, it must come from the inside. Betrayal only occurs when someone you know and love does it. Betrayal means to deliver or expose to an enemy by treachery or disloyalty. Betrayal also means to be unfaithful in guarding. There are many elements of betrayal, but a lack of loyalty is most heinous. Loyalty is not something that we preach a lot from a human stand point. We urge people to be loyal to God, because that makes sense, but if we are going to see something significant grown in our cities, we need people that are loyal to us. Loyalty is a prerequisite for leadership. If you are not loyal to the vision and senior leadership of a house, you can not serve there. Allowing someone to serve, without adequate time to test their loyalty, is a mistake. Judas was one of the disciples of Jesus. Judas was trusted and given great responsibility.

> *For some of them thought, because Judas had the bag, that Jesus had said unto him, Buy those things that we have need of against the feast; or, that he should give something to the poor. (John 13:29)*

Judas was given the task to protect the money or the treasury. This was a significant role. This job could have gone to Levi, or Matthew, for he was a tax collector and no doubt had financial wisdom and understanding. Jesus gave the oversight of the money to Judas. Why is this?

For where your treasure is, there will your heart be also. (Matthew 6:21)

What Jesus actually gave Judas was his heart. As leaders, this can be a hard thing to do. What betrayal comes to do is eliminate your ability to trust. Once a leader's ability to trust is broken, the vision is arrested and goes nowhere. Church planter, it is impossible to share your vision with people you do not trust. Betrayal comes to push leaders into isolation, making them afraid to ever trust again. Jesus gave Judas his heart, and you must too give your heart to people that may very well betray you. You can not be afraid of betrayal. Fear of betrayal will cut off channels of impartation, create an atmosphere of coldness and establish a climate that is not conducive to grow covenant relationships. When leaders are betrayed that become bitter, independent and resentful, always hating the very people they are called to minister to. So many pastors, when finished ministering will run out of the sanctuary to find solitude. This is not always a sign of pride, but could be a sign of brokenness. Pastors are betrayed time and time again, and still have to minister to the same people who cry "crucify him, crucify him." Betrayal comes to birth distrust within a house, which will, if unchecked, produce division. I think it is interesting to note that money was the motivating factor. I do not believe it is wise to hire someone who has a money problem. People who are looking for a paycheck tend to go to great odds to get more money. Greed is a dangerous spirit. Greed will lead people to break lifelong relationships, just for a check. Betrayal comes to make everyone suspicious of each other, destroying any hope of authentic relationships or fellowship.

Vision must be established, casted, carried, protected and grown. To grow vision, we have to develop a culture calibrated to grow the vision. Vision is great, but it cannot survive without culture. Culture is what develops the vision to the point of manifestation.

Here are some tips to developing vision:
1. Spending quality and consistent alone time with Jesus.
2. Writing down key words and phrases that explain or detail the vision.
3. Focusing on the picture that God shows you of the end.
4. Finding and surrounding yourself with people that you can share your vision with.
5. Write the vision down, and meditate on it, bringing it to life.
6. Create a vision board. Find pictures, colors or anything that reminds you of the vision.
7. Pray. Pray. Pray. As you pray, God births the vision.

Greenhouses and Habitats

Chapter Five

Growing the Culture of your Church

Vision is important, but culture is critical. Vision is needed, but culture is a necessity. Vision produces leaders, but the right culture grows legends. Vision is where we are going, but culture gets me to my destination. Vision shows me the picture, but culture grows the vision. We often forget how important our environment is. There are few things that can overpower an environment. It is hard not to become something that you are always surrounded by. Culture produces a church with the environment to grow certain types of fruit, and by fruit I mean believers. Every city has a certain appetite. Every city has certain dietary needs. It is our job as planters, to diagnose the diets of our cities and then grow what they need. What determines what you grow? It is the culture of your house. Remember, vision can many times be very vaporous or intangible, but culture is what people see, feel, and experience every time they walk through the doors of your ministry. In this chapter, we want to define culture and discuss its dynamics, but we also want to deal with the 12 Cultures that must be established in every house.

What is culture? Culture is the sum total of attitudes, customs, and beliefs that distinguish one family, tribe, or house from another. It is what a family does, and the way they do it. Culture is what makes a house distinct and unique. Culture is our flavor. Flavors are complex. We are not just dealing with salty, sweet, and bitter flavors, but we are dealing with complex dishes formulated by an array of flavors and spices. Did you know that you have your own flavor? Your gift, anointing, and ministry, has its own distinct flavor. This is why it is dangerous to taste another man's ministry and try to recreate or duplicate it. Most churches don't have their own distinct flavor. It seems as if we live in a day where all ministries taste the same. If you have tasted one, it seems as if you have tasted them all. People are bored with church because there is no variety. We are not all called to grow the same thing, or to do ministry the same way. We are called to grow a distinct culture that cultivates the fruit that out particular region needs.

The word "culture" comes from the Latin word *colo*, with its root meaning "to cultivate," generally refers to patterns of human activity and the symbolic structures that give such activity significance. Culture can also be understood as the values, norms or structures that give a group their identity. So when we deal with the culture of a house, we are dealing with what is normal in that ministry. These things don't just happen, they must be grown intentionally. Churches rarely align their culture with their vision. They are in the country, trying to grow an urban ministry. They're an entirely African American congregation trying to have a multicultural ministry, but sing nothing but traditional gospel music. The vision and the culture must be aligned to see growth.

Culture is made up of three things: values, norms and structures. When we deal with value, we are talking about what is important. It is hard to build culture when you do not have core values. Every ministry should take time to contemplate on what is most important to their ministry. This will usually stem from what is most important to the Senior Leader. The core values of a house become the blueprint or DNA, the very building blocks of culture. What are your core values? For example, our core values are such:

Core Values
1. Vision
2. Order
3. Prayer
4. Family
5. Reconciliation
6. Faith

7. Diversity
8. Unity
9. Worship
10. Prosperity
11. Servanthood
12. Cultural Engagement
13. Leadership

These thirteen core values dictate everything that we do, and everything that we will ever be involved in. The core values form our identity. If you have not yet formulated your core values, do that now. Ask yourself these questions:

1. What is important to me?
2. What are my non-negotiables?
3. What can I do without?
4. What should our focus be?

As you are led of the Lord, these questions become the foundation of your assignment. Core values are meant to ground you, and make you stable, so that you won't change with the seasons and become a fad. Core values also help develop your doctrinal focus and your teaching curriculum. Your core values will determine what is important in your house. As you teach on your values and impart them through word and deed, all of a sudden relationships are solidified and forged in a supernatural way. When a house is bound together by core values, they can survive the storms and wars of ministry. We have to ask ourselves the hard question, "Why are people attracted to us?" If people are attracted to your preaching, when you don't preach they won't be there. If people are attracted to your worship, if you sing a song they don't like, they will leave. People must become a part of your community based on the core values they share with you. Culture is about value. What do you value the most? When shaping your values, we must be balanced and not overemphasize a particular thing. This produces lopsided ministries, cultish in their beliefs, and inflexible in their perspectives.

Culture is not just values, but norms. Simply put, norms are what we perceive as normal. In some nations, men beating women is normal. To see a man put his hands on a woman wouldn't produce a second glance. In some churches a lack of generosity is normal. In an effort not to push the envelop on money, they rarely mention it, let alone ask for it or teach about it. In some places dishonor is normal. They don't recognize gifts, anointing or rank. Why am I saying this? I want you to understand that norms vary from society to society, and even from house to house. In some houses, a child speaking disrespectfully to their parents is tolerated. If you came from a house like mine, speaking disrespectfully could have gotten you killed. Norms vary from place to place. What is normal here may not be normal there. You have to decide what you want normal to look like in your church. What is normal will dictate the behavior and outlook of your people. I have been to churches that consistently start thirty minutes behind schedule, and then get upset when people show up late. What ministries rarely realize is that we condition the congregants through consistent actions. Most places, in order to enforce their norms, create laws. Laws are meant to govern the norms of a society. I think developing "Do's and Don'ts" statements will help you clarify this. Look at this example:

1. We DO give
2. We DO love
3. We DO growth
4. We DO worship
5. We DON'T judge
6. We DON'T spectate
7. We DON'T show up late

Simple statements like these pinpoint your norms and help you create a concise model to give to your leaders. While your values are usually inwardly carried, your norms are outwardly displayed. Norms become great indicators for you to identify those who are visitors or travelers from another house. When people come to your church, but they don't do what you do, this is an opportunity to expose them to something they have never seen. No one wants to be the odd ball, so the norms help to create an environment that pressures anything that is not like your house to conform. This is not a bad thing; it is essential in building culture. We must ask that everyone adopt the same norms, otherwise we won't be able to hold everyone to the same standard.

> *I beseech you therefore, brethren, by the mercies of God, that ye present your bodies a living sacrifice, holy, acceptable unto God, which is your reasonable service. 2 And be not conformed to this world: but be ye transformed by the renewing of your mind, that ye may prove what is that good, and acceptable, and perfect, will of God. (Romans 12:1-2)*

I wanted to use this scripture to deal with the concept of conforming. As a minister you are building something, and in order to mold and shape lives, it takes pressure. The scripture speaks of being predestined to conform into the image of Jesus (Romans 8:29). The word "conformed" there is the Greek word *suschematizo*. This word "conformed" literally means to be formed, fashioned, or squeezed into the image of another, especially one's mind or character. God does not want us to be conformed to this world, but He does want us to be conformed into the image of His Son. It is impossible for people to become a part of the family without conforming. We celebrate everyone's uniqueness and authenticity, but there is a blessing in unity, not of style, but substance. As new people join your ministry, they must be conformed into the image of that ministry, otherwise they will never fit in, and form covenant relationships, which are the anchors that keep people planted.

Culture is also structure. Cultures are also identified by traditions and customs. In most cultures there are days observed, dialects that fill living rooms, and stories that only the family understands. Cultures are defined by what we think is sacred. The God we worship, and the traditions that mark our allegiance, define our culture. I remember as a young man that we were taught not to speak loud in cemeteries. Anytime we were around a cemetery, even if we were just driving past, we would all be silent. These types of traditions become what our cultures are identified by. People know us by our traditions. Traditions, on a national scale, are often called customs. Every house has customs. A custom is a traditional and widely accepted way of behaving or doing something that is specific to a particular society, place, or time. Can you identify some customs within your local church?

GROWING CULTURE

Culture, like a church, must be planted and grown. Let us begin to deal with the process of growing culture. First understand the importance of culture. Without culture nothing can be grown. The purpose of planting is growth. When we are dealing with growing culture, it all begins with actions. While vision begins with words, culture begins with actions. Bishop Michael Pitts, in his book, *Power Shifters*, releases an incredible concept on Atmospheres and Climates. I used that teaching, implemented and remixed it. The results were phenomenal and we have taught this in our church, Embassy International, since our inception.

1. Actions produce Atmospheres
2. Atmospheres sustained create Climates
3. Climates maintained form Cultures

Actions produce Atmospheres

Everything that we do has vibrations. Everything that we say causes a ripple effect. These vibrations or ripples, also called consequences, help shape the world that we live in. The effect of our actions, thoughts, words and the like, creates an atmosphere. Actions produce atmospheres. For example, you are having a great day, and all of a sudden someone does the wrong thing, it can totally shift your atmosphere. One action changed your atmosphere.

> *To appoint unto them that mourn in Zion, to give unto them beauty for ashes, the oil of joy for mourning, the garment of praise for the spirit of heaviness; that they might be called trees of righteousness, the planting of the LORD, that he might be glorified. (Isaiah 61:3)*

124

This is a very familiar verse of scripture. We usually reference this verse when we are trying to create an atmosphere for praise. This scripture tells us to put on the garments of praise for the spirit of heaviness. Heaviness can be translated depression, sadness or even guilt and shame. We are to put on, like a garment, praise. What does this mean? The same way a garment covers our entire body, praise is supposed to cover our entire body. Every part of our body must be engaged in praise to break heaviness. The action of praise is the remedy for depression. Why? It shifts the atmosphere. Depression can not survive in an atmosphere of fun, laughter, and joy. The only thing that can strengthen depression is more depression. Atmospheres are powerful. An atmosphere is defined as the envelope of gases surrounding the earth or another planet. In our context, it is that feeling that surrounds a ministry or leader. Atmospheres are also known as the pervading tone or mood of a place, situation, or work of art. The atmosphere in a house is produced by the actions of those in top tier leadership. Every action that we make has a profound effect on the house that we serve in. As you are planting, always remember that people are watching your every move. If you don't like this, quit now. When Adam sinned, it immediately shifted his atmosphere. Not only was he ejected from Eden, but also he was translated out of a garden, and into a forest, this is why Adam was hiding behind trees. The same way that negative actions have a negative effect on our atmosphere, so does positive actions have a positive effect on our houses.

Since actions create atmospheres, actions take on a different level of influence now. Every action must be strategic, systematic, and in line with the destiny of that ministry. The Senior Leader has a unique and obligatory role when it comes to setting the atmosphere. Since actions are in abundance, without any distinction, it is easy for a house to become confused and lack unity if actions are neither praised nor corrected. Every action must be praised or corrected in order to establish a code of conduct. Understand that this takes time, and it is a process that you have to be patient with. Church planters must be very watchful, understanding that any haphazard action can become a catalyst for failure in the future.

Atmospheres sustained create Climates

Once we figure out the right actions that produce the atmosphere we want, it is now our duty to be consistent in those actions, so that the atmosphere is sustained. It is only a sustained atmosphere that becomes a climate. Atmospheres come and go, and many times are too weak to grow anything of substance. An atmosphere of contention can cause a fight, but a hostile climate can grow hateful people. A fight can be forgiven, but hatred eats at the core of a person's personality.

Climate is the weather conditions prevailing in an area in general or over a long period of time. We understand this within the context of geography. There are six major climates in the world: polar, temperate, arid, tropical, mediterranean, and tundra. Though the weather of an area can change daily, when seen for longer periods of time, it shows a general pattern of climate. For example, though it may rain on some days in the tropics and on others in the desert, rainfall is greater and more constant in the tropics. These patterns classify the world into six major climate regions. These six regions are also called biomes. A biome is defined as a complex biotic community characterized by distinctive plant and animal species and maintained under the climatic conditions of the region. Every climate grows a certain community. The community that is grown in that climate is called a biome. What type of community are you trying to grow? What you are trying to grow is depends on the climate that is set in your house. The atmosphere you set determines the climate of your house. Every atmosphere is caused by the actions you affirm and/or correct.

Culture moves your people from a gathering, to a team, and now to a community. Community is the goal of culture. Culture develops high sophisticated communities, complex and distinct systems of life. These cultures are the result of climates. The natural climates form by position and location. In our houses we have the advantage of discovering the fruit God wants us to grow, and then creating a climate that is conducive to grow that fruit.

Climates maintained form Cultures

Once there is a climate set in your house, you will begin to see a culture develop. The culture will reveal itself within the core of your house first. As we discussed earlier, culture is seen through our values, norms and structures.

Culture is everything. Culture is how we speak, how we operate, how we interact. Culture is not just what we do, but how we do it, and how we feel when we do it. Culture is what we do without thinking. Culture is not limited to behavior, but it is undoubtedly seen within our habits. Watching your church's habits is a good way to indicate the culture you have established. While vision can seemingly change over night, it takes time to change culture. This is why culture should be set with caution and care. It is hard to change a bad culture. Businesses and corporations are trying to figure out the mystery of culture to this day. How do we change the very environment of our workplace? The secret to your ministry's success is culture. What is the set environment that you have sanctioned to grow the people you are called to lead? I want to deal with the 12 Cultures every house needs, and then we will discuss different tools to creating these environments.

12 CULTURES EVERY HOUSE NEEDS

As you develop the culture of your house, your ministry becomes a greenhouse of sorts to grow certain types of Believers, certain types of fruit. A greenhouse is a building, room, or area in which the temperature is maintained within a desired range, used for cultivating tender plants or growing plants out of season. In the fast pace cities of the world, the church has become a greenhouse to grow what those cities can't cultivate. Our cities need leaders, our cities need the sound of Heaven, our cities need the breaking power of deliverance, but they can not grow it. As church planters we enter these cities that are pregnant with possibility, and with divine power and strategy, build a greenhouse to grow the impossible. Greenhouses are usually made of glass. Glass is very fragile and delicate, but is transparent, so it allows the amount of sun the plants need to shine through. Glass breaks very easily. The greenhouses that God has called us to erect are not made with glass, for we are not in need of the light that comes from the Sun. We have the divine light.

In him was life; and the life was the light of men. 5 And the light shineth in darkness; and the darkness comprehended it not. (John 1:4-5)

God has given us a divine opportunity to grow something incredible in our cities, but it can not be done without creating the right culture. Culture is the key to growth. While vision may inspire our people, it is culture that creates the right habitat for their development. Many times the plans, purposes and promises of God for our life are aborted because of toxic culture.

TOXIC CULTURE

Before we get into the cultures that will help us grow a house of major impact, it is important that we identify things that contend against our growth. While cultures help us produce, toxic culture makes us barren. Barrenness is when a ministry or gift does not have the ability to be fruitful. Do you remember what God told Adam? God said "Be fruitful," this was a command. Our houses are called to produce, but production can be stifled and stagnated by toxic culture. The word "toxic" means deadly. Toxic culture is anything that does not contribute to the growth and expansion of the vision or people in a place. Toxic culture seeks to kill the vision of a house. Dr. Sam Chand always says "toxic culture will eat great vision for lunch!" Culture can not just be grown, it must be defended.

And the LORD God took the man, and put him into the garden of Eden to dress it and to keep it. (Gen. 2:15)

When God gave the custodianship of the Garden to Adam, God told Adam to do two things: to dress it, and keep it. The word "dress" means to work, till, or expand. The word "dress" can also mean to grow or expand. The Garden was the place of Adam's assignment. The Garden was the platform for his gift, and as he served in this place his platform increased. It is only faithfulness that grows a platform. When a gift is given opportunity, they must be faithful in and with that moment. Adam was commanded to dress the Garden. Adam was also commanded to keep the Garden. The word "keep" is the Hebrew word *shamar*, and it means to watch, guard and/or protect. This is the same command that Jesus gave to the disciples when He was in the Garden praying before His passion. Every garden needs watchers. Every assignment needs guards that steward and defend the integrity of what is growing in that place. Adam was growing something in the Garden of Eden, so was Jesus in the Garden of Gethsemane. Jesus was growing a fruit that the world could eat from, but He needed watchers. Every church needs people who watch for the development of toxic culture. Adam was a defender of the culture of the Kingdom within the Garden, and it was only when he became distracted that something crept in and caused contamination. We need people within the churches that we are planting, which fight to maintain the culture of our houses.

Every church or house needs distinct cultures to grow what their region needs, but there are some cultures that should be found in every 21st century house. I believe that the 12 cultures that we are about to discuss should be developed in every house that will become a formidable force within our society.

It was around the end of 2007 that I ventured out on a quest. After serving for 3 years in different capacities at a local church, I began a journey that would literally change my life. For about two years all I did was visit churches. I looked at big churches and small churches of every ethnicity and financial level. I traveled to churches that were located in the city, in the country, and even churches that were only online. During these studies I became aware of something very shocking. All of the ministries that I attended that were fruitful had certain things in common. These commonalities are what I call the 12 cultures that every house needs. As you develop your own distinct culture and brand, you will add more of your own, but these should remain as pillars to hold up a powerful church. The 12 cultures are:

1. Vision
2. Order
3. Prayer
4. Praise and Worship
5. Prophetic
6. Deliverance
7. Prosperity
8. Grace
9. Empowerment
10. Leadership
11. Faith
12. Supernatural

Each one of these cultures holds a key to the success of a house. These are not unique, but they are needed. You can find other cultures that need to be established in your local house, but these twelve create a formidable foundation to hold ministries of great weight. We will discuss each of these cultures briefly, to give an understanding and a concise definition of each.

Vision

Vision can not just be the God picture of where you are going, but the fuel that drives us forward. Vision must move from verbiage to actual vitality. The culture of vision grows people who live blueprint lives. A blueprint life is a life lived on purpose and by God's design. A church that grows a culture of vision produces people who are always trying to become better. When people constantly reevaluate themselves for the purpose of construction, they enter into cycles of improvement, which results in accelerated maturity. A culture of vision grows people who live for tomorrow. Without the culture of vision, churches remain locked within generations, never creating legacy. Vision demands generational planning, and when we build a culture of vision, we raise up people who plan beyond their life span.

Order

And God hath set some in the church, first apostles, secondarily prophets, thirdly teachers, after that miracles, then gifts of healings, helps, governments, diversities of tongues. (1 Cor. 12:28)

When Paul writes to Corinth his purpose is to set order. In setting order, Paul builds the understanding of rank by saying "first apostles." This statement is vast in its significance. Apostles are anointed and gifted by God to establish order. Adam was an apostolic gift. When the world was in chaos, God raised an apostle. After Adam fell, God raises up another apostle, Jesus Christ (Heb. 3:1). Our Lord's assignment was to restore order according to John's gospel, chapter three and verse sixteen. Whenever there is a lack of order, God raises up an apostle. We need apostles in our cities, in our regions, and especially in our churches. Apostles set order by the force of teaching and the supernatural. Apostles don't just plant churches, but they plant their life.

Let all things be done decently and in order. (1Cor. 14:40)

Order is the right arrangement of things. Without order we have no definition. Without definition, we have the wrong destination. Order is so important because without order we have the breaking of rank. The Kingdom of God functions within four dynamics: order, rank, protocol, and power. Where there is no order, there is no power. Order is literally the correct function of a thing. When there is no order, things can not operate effectively. Have you ever seen a device that was out of order? An out of order sign means that the device does not work properly. When a church does not have order it does not work properly. Our houses must be houses of order if we are going to see transformation in our communities. Most of our neighborhoods are so chaotic, because they have never seen order. Walking into an apostolic house can be a culture shock for most people, because they are seeing rank for the first time. Can you imagine teaching the world the power of God just through our order and excellence? Order produces excellence. Excellence is a byproduct of order. Excellence becomes a testimony to the greatness of our God, and His majesty. The excellence of God attracts the attention of the world, like the Queen of Sheba in Solomon's day.

Prayer

I have found that developing a culture of prayer can be one of the toughest cultures to grow. Usually prayer meetings are scarcely attended. This has to change. The disciples speaking to Jesus had a very significant request,

...Lord, teach us to pray.. (Luke 11:1)

Prayer must be taught. Jesus said, "My house shall be called the house of prayer." The culture of prayer is grown through consistent and intense intercession, which is first modeled by the senior leadership of the house. Prayer energizes the house to receive miracles and walk in power. The culture of prayer, praise, and worship, work together to pull down the atmosphere of Heaven into the Earth. Prayer can not become an event, it must be a lifestyle. Prayer must be a culture that is seen in every facet of our services and ministries. One of the ways you establish this culture is by beginning and ending everything your church does with prayer. One of the ways that we continue to grow the culture of prayer at Embassy International Worship Center is by opening our corporate service with intense corporate prayer. Asking everyone within the congregation to engage in prayer must be a given. You can not let up when it comes to demanding your people to pray. Remember, if they can not pray with you, they can not lead with you.

Praise and Worship

Quiet congregations can not change a city. It takes an exuberant house to shake a city. Praise and worship flows from the place of relationship. This culture is developed as we lift Jesus higher. Jesus said "If you lift me up, I will draw all men unto me." Praise is power. Opening our mouth together in unity, declaring the greatness of our God, has earth shaking ability.

The culture of praise and worship must be strong within a house because it's combating the sound of the world. I will deal with the importance of minstrels and developing the sound of your house in a moment, but praise and worship must be a priority in our house. It is the culture of worship that puts a demand on the relationship that our people have with the Lord Jesus. It is during these intimate moments where our people move into the reality of forgiveness and the blood of Jesus ministers to them. There is nothing that can replace praise and worship. We have been taught that the pinnacle of our time with the Lord is the preaching of His word, but I think that we should restructure our houses so that the zenith of our gathering is the very presence of our God.

Prophetic

Wherever the presence of the Lord is, God is sure to speak to the hearts of men. Growing the culture of the prophetic is difficult in a day where ministries are patterned after circus performances, and rarely have biblical precedent for the antics they display. If the culture of the prophetic is going to be grown, we will need to focus on maturing our people past "television Christianity." A prophetic culture is a culture in which there is freedom for God to move in a way that pleases him. God loves to interrupt lives, disrupt services, and surprise sinners with His goodness.

Despise not prophesyings. (1 Thess. 5:20)

It is the prophetic that releases life within a house. If God is not speaking, the church you are planting is nothing more than a valley of dry bones. Prophesy releases the wind of the Lord to blow on the entire church and activate them into their destiny. A church can not survive with a living, breathing, and vibrant word from the Lord.

But he answered and said, It is written, Man shall not live by bread alone, but by every word that proceedeth out of the mouth of God. (Matt. 4:4)

A house can not survive on bread alone, which is doctrine; it needs the very voice of the Lord.

3 The voice of the LORD is upon the waters: the

God of glory thundereth: the LORD is upon many waters. 4 The voice of the LORD is powerful; the voice of the LORD is full of majesty. 5 The voice of the LORD breaketh the cedars; yea, the LORD breaketh the cedars of Lebanon. 6 He maketh them also to skip like a calf; Lebanon and Sirion like a young unicorn. 7 The voice of the LORD divideth the flames of fire. 8 The voice of the LORD shaketh the wilderness; the LORD shaketh the wilderness of Kadesh. 9 The voice of the LORD maketh the hinds to calve, and discovereth the forests: and in his temple doth every one speak of his glory. (Psalm 29:3-9)

This is a powerful display of the ability of God's voice. This psalm gives us a detailed understanding of the purpose of the Lord's voice. It says that the voice of the Lord is,

1. **The voice of the Lord is upon the waters**- this gives us an idea of how the voice of the Lord is released. Waves of the water come to and fro. Waves are consistent, but not constant, there is a difference. As waves of the sea come in, they restructure the shores and boundaries of our life.
2. **The voice of the Lord is powerful and full of majesty**- the voice of the Lord is raw power. The voice of the Lord is raw transformative ability. The voice of the Lord has the ability to change any situation. This is why we need the prophetic in our houses, because without it people will remain the same. It also says that the voice of God is full of majesty, royal authority, and power. We must create a culture of reverence towards the word of God. One of the ways to develop this standard is by having people stand during the reading of the word, and trying to discourage walking during the preaching of the word of God.
3. **The voice of the Lord breaks**- the word of God has delivering power and has the ability to break through any limitation.
4. **The voice of the Lord divides the flames of fire**- Flames of fire are often spoken of in reference to ministers of the gospel. It is the word of God that awakens man's ear to hear

the calling of the Lord. It is the preaching of the word of God that pricks the hearts of men, and brings them to the saving knowledge of Jesus Christ.

5. **The voice of the Lord shakes the wilderness**- the wilderness is the place of testing and filtering. We see this with Jesus, during the days of His temptation. We also see the purpose of the wilderness with the children of Israel as they left Egypt. The word "shake" literally means to dance. The voice of the Lord comes to give us hope in days of heat. The word of God gives us the ability to navigate through tough times in our life.

6. **The voice of the Lord maketh the hinds to calve**- this literally means that it strips things bear. The word of God has revealing ability. The scripture says that the word of God is sharp, having the ability to reveal thoughts and intents. When this happens, everyone in the temple shouts "glory!"

The culture of the prophetic is so important to the development of a 21st century house, without it, we cannot offer the world the wisdom of God. We need prophetic ability, for by it our future is revealed, and our present is made perfect.

Deliverance

The culture of deliverance should not be confused with the manifestations of deliverance. What do I mean? A culture of deliverance can also be called a culture of healing. Within a culture of deliverance everyone seeks to better themselves by identifying iniquitous patterns and breaking generational curses. Deliverance can have a variety of manifestations. Screaming, crying, yelling, falling out, yawning and sneezing can all be manifestation of demonic activity during the deliverance process, but a culture of deliverance transcends just its manifestation.

In our houses, people must be acquainted with the delivering power of God. Altar calls are not a thing of the past; they are very much needed in the church today. We must expect deliverance to occur during prayer, praise and worship, the preaching or the word, and during giving. We must have faith that at any given moment, God can set the captives free.

Prosperity

In order for churches to make a significant deposit within the communities they are planted in, we have to create a culture of generosity. Giving is a taboo subject, and even within the Body of Christ there are people that agree and disagree with the issue of tithing. That is not a subject I will go into now, but it will suffice to say that giving has always been apart of the culture of the Kingdom.

We encourage giving during our entire service at Embassy International. Some people give at the beginning, some give during the preaching of the word, and then we have a corporate time for giving. A culture of prosperity breeds generous people who will stop at nothing to become a blessing. This was the promise that God made to Abraham, that He would make Abraham a blessing. God wants our church to be a blessing to the city we are planted in, but the only way we can do that is if we challenge people to be ridiculous givers. Giving must be taught, preached, sung, prophesied, and encouraged. We must make giving easy within the house of God by creating as many ways as possible for people to give. We want to be able to offer as many services to the community as possible free of charge. When we are able to bless our region with no strings attached, because our people have been grown in a culture of generosity, it radically shifts their mentality about the church and the love of God.

Grace

There are many people that pervert the gospel of grace. Churches that overemphasize an unbalanced view of grace create clubs of chaos. The message of grace is the most powerful message that we can preach. We have been made ministers of reconciliation and restoration. Grace must be preached not just radically, but biblically. A church that has been saturated with grace will be strong and do great exploits. It is grace that brings a supernatural boldness into a house and really energizes the areas of prayer, praise and worship, and giving.

Growing a culture of grace means you intentionally love

beyond limits, and you forgive without measure. Every house needs corrective systems, but when there is a culture of grace, men will repent willingly without hesitation. A culture of grace is a culture of forgiveness. A culture of grace is where we minimize your faults and magnify your strengths. Grace is the culture that becomes the foundation of dramatic and supernatural salvations. The Bible says that it is the goodness of the Lord that brings men to repentance (Romans 2:4).

Developing a culture of grace isn't easy. Men are fragile and flesh is always an issue when you are dealing with human beings. Grace gives us the ability to deal with disappointment and sin, which you will encounter a lot. Sin won't just be an issue in the pew, but it will touch every area of your church, including senior leadership. But, when there is a culture of grace, everyone knows how to deal with sin and disobedience. When you are growing this culture, it is important to understand that you have a responsibility to protect people. While you must forgive all, this doesn't mean that you have to be naive when it comes to people's character and/or behavior. Some people make it easy for you not to trust them. You should not appoint these people into areas of leadership. Burdens should only be given to those who have proved themselves dependable. We have had several cases within our church where breaches were made relationally, that could not be mended, and although we forgave them, we could no longer work together. The culture of grace should not make your congregation susceptible to destructive cycles, but should be a radical display of the love of God. Grace releases people from the bondage of judgment, and gives us a sense of accountability and expectation.

Empowerment

I remember as a kid when I would go to church, I would leave feeling worse than I did when I arrived. The Kingdom of God is about empowerment, not condemnation. Our role in the community is to empower the people to become all that God has called them to be. Empowerment is the force to succeed. The culture of empowerment is an environment that makes everyone feel like they can do anything. This is a culture filled with hope and expectation, but also responsibility to continue to expand and grow. For so long our preaching, teaching, and even singing have locked people within bubbles of mediocrity. We are quick to tell people how minuscule and broken they are, failing to realize the supernatural ability of empowerment. When Jesus walked the earth, people came to Him for healing and wholeness, but on many occasions He gave them a command of empowerment.

I say unto thee, Arise, and take up thy bed, and go thy way into thine house. (Mark 2:11)

Jesus did not want the empowerment of people to stop with Him, as a matter of fact, on one occasion Jesus said, "you will do greater works than I have done." As you grow a culture of empowerment, you challenge people to out do what they have always done, to set and break personal records. When we build a culture of empowerment, people are strengthened to reach their potential. Empowerment is about education. You can not empower people without strong teaching. The day for noise without substance is over. If we are going to be a culture of empowerment, we must inform people and keep them up to date with current affairs and events. You can not empower people and keep them ignorant.

Leadership

Whenever you empower people, you will naturally pull out the leader in them. Everyone has a leader in them, and when you develop a culture of leadership, you are intentionally targeting that place of authority. Most ministries focus on our broken pieces, because we do need healing, but if we never speak to the leader in people they will remain dependent on us.

Raising up leaders is what we are called to do. We are not to handicap people, or make the church a crutch for people to lean on for their entire life. We are to activate the leader in everyone, causing them to be a force of inspiration to their spheres of influence. A culture of leadership can be grown through specialized classes, seminars, and events geared towards leadership subjects such as: financial planning, teaching dynamics, starting businesses and investing. As you create a culture of leadership, everyone takes the responsibility of carrying the burden of the vision, and you will find that the weight of the church becomes more evenly distributed.

Faith

Faith is Kingdom action. Moving in the Kingdom of God requires faith. Without faith, there is no movement in the Kingdom. When a house has little faith, people will stay in the boats of comfortability, never pushing on the limits. They will be rigid in their creativity, exploits, and programs. Faithless churches are churches that rarely do anything that captivates the attention of the world. Faithless churches become memorials in the communities they are planted in. Like fossils, they are set to remind us of the past. God is raising faith-filled churches, who with great passion, walk on the water of the impossible, pushing the envelop in every way. When you are building a culture of faith, other churches will excommunicate you, and deem you too wild or too unconventional. A culture of faith is the perfect environment to raise risk takers and history makers. You do not want a church filled with status quo people. The culture of faith challenges everyone to do something extraordinary. Most churches only deal with faith during capital campaigns or strenuous building projects, but by this time it is too late to muster up the faith you need to break through. Faith must be taught, preached, and demonstrated as an active ingredient in your house. Planting a church requires faith, and without a culture of faith, enthusiasm will subside and people will not have the ability to continue with you. People can only go as far as their faith. A culture of faith raises our people's endurance and stamina to outlast the difficult times that are sure to come during planting anything significant.

Growing a culture of faith takes faith. You have to constantly challenge the congregation to do things that go against statistics and make no logical sense. A church that is intentional about growing a culture of faith will put unusual demands on the people, and believe they will rise to the occasion. You must be careful while establishing this culture, making sure you don't focus on the results alone, but more so on the journey. Faith is not just about the outcome, it is about the growth you encounter as a result of believing. Doubt cannot live in a culture of faith.

> *Again I say unto you, That if two of you shall agree on earth as touching any thing that they shall ask, it shall be done for them of my Father which is in heaven. (Matt. 18:19)*

Supernatural

The supernatural comes as a result of developing the cultures of faith, the prophetic, praise, and worship. These cultures converge to create a supernatural habitat for miracles, signs, and wonders. A church without the supernatural is nothing more than a glorified club without benefits. The culture of the supernatural actually produces a church that has a heart for the lost and broken. Evangelism as a responsibility is always ineffective, but as a byproduct of an encounter with Jesus, it will always yield much fruit. The culture of the supernatural is developed by teaching and preaching, but more so, through demonstration. Demonstration and demand is the key to growing a culture of the supernatural.

DEVELOPING THE SOUND OF THE HOUSE

When we begin to speak about the sound of the house, we are talking about the distinct sound that a house makes. Every voice has a distinct sound and print. The sound of the house is the distinct sound and vocal print of that corporate body. There is nothing that develops culture like sound. Putting your vision, culture, and purpose to sound helps to plant the ministry in the hearts of the congregants. The sound of the house is developed and maintained by the minstrels and psalmists of the house. A minstrel is one who is skilled and anointed, one who is called to release the sound of Heaven in the Earth, while psalmists do the same, only with their vocal ability. Please understand that the culture of your house is established faster by music than by your message. You can preach until your mouth is dry, but when you put the vision to music, people will be able to remember it long after they forget the message. The ministry of psalmists and minstrels cannot be overlooked. How much time do you spend developing the Sound of the House?

During the formation stages of your house, you must be very specific with your minstrels and psalmist as it relates to the sound you are trying to build. Haphazardly allowing people to select songs because of their popularity is a big mistake. Songs must be carefully chosen according to the culture of the house. Many times our worship and arts departments choose songs that are on the radio, or songs that are easily recognized. Until we shift the focus of our worship from people to the presence, we won't see real glory in our houses. Minstrels and psalmists must spend quality time with each other to develop strategies that will effectively enable them to work together within a house.

The word "psalmist" in the Hebrew is the word *zamiyr*. This word literally means a song, but by revelation, this word means a master at songs. A psalmist is one who is a master at songs, and can shift atmospheres. Psalmists must be sons. When you have multiple psalmists releasing a sound in a ministry, without covenant or connection to the vision, a sustainable atmosphere can not be produced. Psalmists must be loyal, and more concerned with growing a culture of worship, than furthering their own musical career. Most church platforms have become Pre-American Idol auditions and practice grounds for those hoping to make it big. Churches struggle with developing a consistent sound because worship and arts departments have been high jacked by hirelings. A psalmist must have the pastor's heart, and become a guardian of their anointing and mood through their gift. David, when called to the palace of Saul, was given an assignment to minister to the King, not the Kingdom. The first job of the psalmist is to the set man or woman, not to the church. The psalmist should understand their responsibility to sooth the mood of the pastor, and create a suitable atmosphere for him or her to minister. Psalmists do this with the help of minstrels.

The word "minstrel" in the Hebrew, is the word *nagan*, and it literally means to "strike the string," which gives us an understanding of warfare. The minstrel is a warrior. This is what David meant, when he said, "teach my hands to war, and my fingers to fight" (Psalm 144:1). Usually minstrels are prophets, but only a few prophets are minstrels. Minstrels are very valuable because it takes a certain level of skill to occupy that office. Minstrels must be skilled in their instrument and must be masters at their craft.

As pastors and leaders of Houses we must demand more of our minstrels. Minstrels must be people of commitment and loyalty and not money and opportunity.

> And the key of the house of David will I lay upon his shoulder; so he shall open, and none shall shut; and he shall shut, and none shall open. (Isa. 22:22)

Minstrels have keys. Minstrels have the grace to open the treasures of God's heart. They open places in the Heavens and release sounds never heard before. This is why minstrels must spend adequate time in the presence of the Lord. They must be very careful of their environments and surroundings. Minstrels are sound carriers, so this makes it very easy for them to retain what they hear, and what they are around.
Lucifer was this type of being:

> Thou hast been in Eden the garden of God; every precious stone was thy covering, the sardius, topaz, and the diamond, the beryl, the onyx, and the jasper, the sapphire, the emerald, and the carbuncle, and gold: the workmanship of thy tabrets and of thy pipes was prepared in thee in the day that thou wast created. (Ezek. 28:13)

Lucifer, who is Satan before he fell from Heaven, was covered in jewels. Jewels not only reflect and refract light, but they also capture and release light. Lucifer would go into the presence of God, soak up the light and sound of God, and then go out among the congregation of the Mighty, and release this light and sound, which would cause all of Heaven to fall down and worship. Lucifer did his job so well that he began to think that the praises belonged to him. The minstrel's job is to go into the heights of Heaven, through prayer, worship, and fasting, through meditation and solitude, and then bring and release what they received. Minstrels must be very careful not to get caught up in the hype. While you are a vessel of God, you are not God.

> It came even to pass, as the trumpeters and singers were as one, to make one sound to be heard in praising and thanking the LORD; and when they lifted up their voice with the trumpets and cymbals and instruments of musick, and praised the LORD, saying, For he is good; for his mercy endureth for ever: that then the house was filled with a cloud, even the house of the LORD; So that the priests could not stand to minister by reason of the cloud: for the glory of the LORD had filled the house of God. (2 Chr. 5:13-14)

It says in 2 Chronicles that the minstrels were as one. This deals with unity, not just with each other, but also with the vision and purpose of the House. Minstrels must be careful to be in sync with the vision and purpose of the House. This is why I believe that ideally, a minstrel should be assigned to one house, and stay loyal to that house. If a minstrel is going from house to house, many times, the sounds begin to blend, and the anointing drops. The scripture also says that they made one sound. They weren't showboating, they weren't trying to be the next best thing, their purpose was to present a unified sound so that the people could go into the presence of the Lord. As they did this, the glory filled the House and the priest could not minister, God ministered.

The ministry of psalmists and minstrels cannot be discounted, but should be fully invested in if we are going to develop the sound of the house. Sound is very important. Sound ushers in new movements. The minstrel and psalmist help to establish the culture of Heaven in the Earth in a very real way.

WAITING ROOMS and ROAD RAGE

Chapter Six

What Do You Do While You Are Waiting

In this chapter I want to look at what you do while you are waiting for great things to happen. We are planters. We are not consumed with immediate gratification. Well, that is what we would like to think. One of the reasons planters shut down, close their churches, or give up, is because honestly they didn't think it would take this long. If you are in this for quick success, get out now. Planting is a lifelong commitment that you make with your family, the church, and with the dirt of your city. You must make a vow to toil regardless of how long it takes. Church planters are usually caught off guard with the time it takes to grow a healthy church. You have to remember that planting takes time.

TIMING

While the earth remaineth, seedtime and harvest, and cold and heat, and summer and winter, and day and night shall not cease. (Gen. 8:22)

As long as we are in the Earth, there are certain laws that we are subject to. There are divine moments where these laws are suspended, but many times these laws serve to produce in us the character we need to operate here on this planet. Laws are established to govern actions and movements. One of the laws that God put in place was the Law of Seedtime and Harvest. This law not only governed the Vegetative Kingdom, but every context that involved a seed or a harvest of some kind. When we look at this scripture, we many times separate seed and time, but in actuality it is one word. The Greek word for seedtime is *zera*. The word *zera* literally means a seed, the act of sowing, or offspring. This is significant because the Bible does not separate sowing from the time it takes to see a harvest, because they are one in the same. Sowing includes time, and you cannot separate the two. It is impossible to sow without understanding the element of time. Anything great takes time. If we are going to build houses that transform our communities, it is going to take time. Time is designed to educate, expose, and eliminate.

When Adam was created, he was made in the image and likeness of God. The Hebrew word "God" is *Elohim*. *Elohim* is the creator. This name reveals God as the great builder and architect. It is through this name that God created the Heavens and the Earth, and through a seven day creational process bringing order to the cosmos. When Adam was created, he was made a creative being. Adam had creative power. Adam, like God, could create through his words, his mind, and through his loins. Adam was perfect in his creative ability. Adam was created a full grown man. Adam did not matriculate through a school system, but rather Adam walked with God. Adam was a being of revelation, not mere information. Why am I saying this? Because when Adam fell, he did not just fall from grace and glory, he fell from revelation into information. Information are those facts that are subject and perceived exclusively by our senses. So now Adam has to "learn." After Adam falls, time serves as an educator for Adam. Like us, we learn as time goes by. As we grow older and experience more, we learn valuable lessons that mature us. Time is not the best educator, but it is a teacher nonetheless. Time gives us the privilege and ability to retrospect. Without time we would not be able to peer into the past and examine it, so that we can improve our present and transform our future. Time gives us a unique perspective on our position, understanding that where I am is because of where I came from. In order to be a great planter, we must understand that time is designed to teach. Time teaches us patience.

3 And not only so, but we glory in tribulations also: knowing that tribulation worketh patience; 4 And

patience, experience; and experience, hope:
(Romans 5:3-4)

The word "patience" here means endurance, consistency and faithfulness. All of these words mean nothing outside of the realm of time. Time becomes a great educator even for our leaders. A leader that cannot survive the test of time is a leader that cannot be trusted. Times serves as a platform to disclose the true nature of people. This leads us to the second purpose of time, exposure.

Time is a revealer of motives. Regardless of what people say, allow time to become the filter to show the true intent of their actions. Time exposes things for what they truly are. Time will reveal if you are planting for the right reasons. Time has a way of pushing all of your feelings and emotions to the surface of your life. Time is not just useful for our leaders, but is also very useful for us. Time shows us things about ourselves that would have remained hidden unless our patience was pushed to the limit. Planting puts pressure on every part of you, especially your patience. Time will reveal your weaknesses, as well as your strength. Can I say to you, that you have no idea how much you can handle until pressure comes? Time becomes a great ally and friend in the development of your confidence. It is only when you have handled hell for a prolonged period of time that you can have confidence in your ability. Time is the revealer of the real you. There is nothing that exposes who you really are, like time. Making people wait is a valuable stage of their development. How people handle the wilderness will determine the level of power they have access to. Please understand with all certainty that your ability to manage your patience determine the power you are trusted with. Time will reveal pride, arrogance and entitlement. It is nothing that can break pride, like time. Time humbles you, because we are all subject to it. There is nothing more sobering than realizing you only have a set amount of time. Time is the great equalizer. We are all finite beings. We will all die one day, and time gives us the benefit of this perspective. Time shows us that none of us will live forever, and this makes the completion of our assignments all the more important and critical.

The third thing that time does is eliminate. Time not only educates and exposes, it also eliminates. Time becomes very strategic within warfare because it weeds out the weak. Exposure always leads to elimination. When our weaknesses are exposed, it is for the purpose of confrontation. Everything that time exposes must be confronted. You will be surprised how many people leave when the time element is introduced. Elimination is important to advancing.

> Wherefore seeing we also are compassed about with so great a cloud of witnesses, let us lay aside every weight, and the sin which doth so easily beset us, and let us run with patience the race that is set before us (Hebrews 12:1)

Ministries can move very slowly when there is the presence of uncommitted people. Many ministries and churches are behind divine schedule because they are carrying extra weight and baggage. Can I suggest to you that people can sometimes be extra weight? We have to be discerning about the people on our staff and teams because each of them comes with weight. When was the last time you did a weight check on your team? Weight checks must be done periodically to evaluate if there is sin, offense, discontent, or murmuring within our leader structure. When there is extra weight, it will take a longer time for us to complete our task. Time helps to eliminate those who are not for us, and helps to identify those who are called into higher levels of leadership.

Time is a part of the program of planting. Becoming an overnight success is one of the worst tricks of the Kingdom of Darkness. Time gives us the opportunity to develop maturity, stewardship, and strategy on how to handle seasons. The Bible says of Jesus,

> And the child grew, and waxed strong in spirit, filled with wisdom: and the grace of God was upon him. (Luke 2:40)

> And Jesus increased in wisdom and stature, and in favour with God and man. (Luke 2:52)

Jesus grew. This only makes since within the dimension of time. Church planter, time is on your side, but it is going to test everything about you. We must see time as a great opportunity to grow. Even Jesus, who was all God, and all man, had to grow. As planters we are called to grow. Growth takes time. Whether you are growing a church, a family, a gift or anointing, it takes time. I have found that there are 12 significant time periods that we interact with.

Different Types of Time:

1. Right Time
2. Wrong Time
3. Set Time
4. Due Time
5. Out of Due Time
6. Ahead of Time
7. Behind Time
8. Right On Time
9. Seasons
10. Chronos
11. Ages or Dispensation
12. Eternity

These 12 time zones help us navigate through life and give us insight into the dynamics of growth. As planters, our concern is with harvest. In order for harvest to come, we must steward our time well. How we manage time will directly determine the success of our harvest. Let us look at, very basically, each one of these time zones.

RIGHT TIME

When I refer to the right time, I am talking about an appropriate time. The right time can be both subjective and objective, but it is a moment of opportunity. Failure occurs when we do the wrong thing at the right time, or when we do the right thing at the wrong time. Success happens when the right thing is done at the right time. The right time is an honorable time.

Those who called to plant the extraordinary and see the impossible grow have to really seek the right time to move. Church planting is a calling, which means that we move by the voice of the Lord. We have to be careful to move by His voice, and not our ambition. Many future leaders abort the possibility of success because they launch out at the wrong time. Having a great idea at the wrong time can be frustrating, but it is the story of all great people. Everyone great has had to wait at some point. As a young pastor and church planter, I have many stories I could tell about the right time. I knew when I was eight years old that I would pastor, but I did not move. At 18 I was licensed, and even then, at the inception of my ministry, I knew I was called to plant, but I didn't move. Even after I became a youth pastor, then college pastor, then associate pastor, and even an executive pastor, I still did not move. Why? Timing is everything. When it comes to planting, timing is everything. You don't plant at any time, you plant during the right time. What am I saying? Seek God for the right time. Let me frustrate you even more. The right time is rarely the time when you receive inspiration. This can be a hard pill to swallow. For pioneers, visionaries, and leaders, we want to move as soon as we get the idea. You have to get an idea for tomorrow, but continue to work the word you have for today. This is an extremely pressurized place of development. You have to be comfortable with "this," knowing that the "that" is so much better. Remember, this is a test.

WRONG TIME

The wrong time is exactly the opposite of the right time. The wrong time is not an opportune time. The wrong time is not an honorable time. The wrong time usually creates more problems than it does solutions. Now many may think that this is a sign from God. I do not know why we think that storms are signs from God. God uses storms, but for Jonah, it was a sign of disobedience. Every storm is not a sign of sin, but moving during the wrong time will always produce storms. We know that all things work together for them who love God, but if you can avoid a shipwreck by moving at the right time, why move at the wrong time? The wrong time is usually before assignments are completed and/or times where seasons are not ripe. I have spoken to countless young leaders who wanted to launch out, but their senior leadership did not believe it was time. In cases like these you have two options, you can leave without approval or blessing, or wait. Waiting when you think you should be moving is very hard to do, but it is needed for your development. If you have not developed the ability to wait when you want to move, you will not be very useful in the Kingdom of God.

> 22 But the fruit of the Spirit is love, joy, peace, longsuffering, gentleness, goodness, faith, 23 Meekness, temperance: against such there is no law. (Galatians 5:22-23)

The scripture is where we get the understanding and revelation of the Fruit of the Spirit. These fruits are grown by the Holy Spirit to make sure the Believer has the character and nature of Christ. One of these fruits listed in verse 23 is the fruit of temperance. Temperance is self-control, or discipline. A disciple is one who is disciplined. Discipline is something that we rarely focus on, which is the reason we have so many undisciplined disciples. Discipline is developed when your actions no longer rely on your emotions, but is fueled by your destiny and purpose. Discipline is when you do something, not based on feeling, but based on habit. The wrong time helps to develop discipline. Can you serve when you are tired? Can you operate lower then you are called for the purpose of advancing the Kingdom? Can you do what you do, without recognition, and without a title? These questions must be answered before the right time opens up for you. The wrong time is a great place to be in. Maybe you are in this place, rejoice, God is building and shaping you into a true disciple.

SET TIME

> ...for the time to favour her, yea, the set time, is come. (Psalm 102:13)

The concept of a set time is seen throughout the scriptures. This word and/or phrase is mentioned in some way, about 23 times in the King James Version of the Bible. The Hebrew word for "set time" is *mowed* (mow-ed), which means an appointed place or an appointed time. This word also carries with it the connotation of a feast, a sacred moment or time, or a sign. This word can also mean a meeting place. The set time is the time appointed for you to meet up with God's promise for your life. We see this in the life of Abraham and Sarah. You know that Sarah was barren; her matrix was malfunctioning, so God says to Abraham, "I will make you a father."

> *But my covenant will I establish with Isaac, which Sarah shall bear unto thee at this set time in the next year. (Gen. 17:21)*

God told Abraham that the covenant would be established, or the promise would be fulfilled at the set time. The set time is the time of promise. There is a time already scheduled in the calendar of Heaven for you to meet, face to face, the promises of God over your life. Notice this word connotes a meeting. Set times can be disappointed if you are not in the right position and/or location. Do you remember when Adam fell? God came in the Garden and asked, "Adam, where are you," why? Because of sin, Adam was no longer in the right location, he was out of position, and therefore the time of meeting was disappointed. Set times that are accessed behind schedule usually spoil and become wrong times. Set times must be sought for manifestations of promises. I have learned through pastoring that some people have never seen an authentic promise fulfilled in their life. One of the reasons people miss the promise of God is because set times are not discerned. When you hit a set time, there is nothing the enemy can do to stop the blessings of God from overtaking your life. Whether you know it or not, the enemy is always trying to knock you off course so that your set times are disappointed.

DUE TIME

> *To me belongeth vengeance, and recompence; their foot shall slide in due time: for the day of their calamity is at hand, and the things that shall come*

upon them make haste. (Deut. 32:35)

Due time is similar to set time. The difference between set time and due time can be understood by understanding the birth of a baby. A baby is only born when it is due. A set time is the date on the calendar they tell you that your child is going to be born, but in actuality it's not guaranteed. The baby could come at any moment, but it's what we call a due time. The due time is when the baby is full term. The due time is when a thing has fulfilled its obligation for the season it's in, and then the baby pushes it's way out. Due time is engaged when you have fulfilled the requirements within a season. Once you have met all the requirements, a due time appears.

> *For when we were yet without strength, in due time Christ died for the ungodly. (Rom. 5:6)*

> *Humble yourselves therefore under the mighty hand of God, that he may exalt you in due time:*
> *(1 Peter 5:6)*

Notice that the scripture in Romans tells us that Christ died in due time. It was not just a set time on the calendar of God, but also a due time. Christ fulfilled the requirements of the law, and at that point it was due time. There were things that had to be done in order for the time to be right for Christ to die. If this was not true Christ could have died at anytime, but it had to be due time. Due time involves waiting.

OUT OF DUE TIME

> *And last of all he was seen of me also, as of one born out of due time. (1 Cor. 15:8)*

While Christ was on the earth, He chose 12 men. After Judas betrayed Jesus, and fell away, the apostles chose Mathias to replace him. It was after this that Paul had his encounter with Jesus on the Damascus road. It may seem like all has been said and all has been done, but we serve a God that can do things off schedule. Paul is an example of God's sovereignty. This realm of time is where God shows the ability of His omnipotence to step outside of the calendar and the agenda and do something amazing. The word that encapsulates this concept is the Greek word *ektroma*. This word, *ektroma*, literally means to be aborted, an abortive birth, or an untimely birth. See Paul did not walk with Jesus, like the rest of the apostles. Paul was not there when Jesus was baptized, crucified, or during His resurrection. Jesus called Paul personally, after Jesus' ascension. After the earthly ministry of Jesus was ended, then was Paul called. Since Christ died at due time, Paul was called out of, or after due time. God is able to do things that are not on his calendar. Do you remember John chapter 2? Jesus was at a wedding at Cana, and the wedding had run out of wine. Jesus was clear that His time had not yet come, but nevertheless at the behest of His mother, He turned the water into wine. Even though it was not time, God did the impossible. You may be feeling like your church, and/or idea is not ready, and cannot grow yet, but great things are born out of due time. Paul went on to become the most famous and prolific apostle to date.

AHEAD, BEHIND, and RIGHT ON TIME

Being syncopated with the plan of God is important. Ambition makes us run in front of God; while entitlement makes us remain at places that God has forgotten about. We need to seek balance within our theological approach to time.

> *Order my steps in thy word: and let not any iniquity have dominion over me. (Psalm 119:133)*

> *For ever, O LORD, thy word is settled in heaven. (Psalm 119:89)*

The Psalmist cries out for God to order his steps in the word of God. Have you ever been to a drive thru restaurant? You pull up to the menu, and there are already prearranged packages and meals to choose from. Your job is to choose what you want from the menu, wait, then pay, and take your order. The Psalmist says, when you order my steps, please do it from the right menu, which is the word of God. Now the psalmist also says that this menu has been established in Heaven. What am I trying to get at? Your steps are already planned out. Before you got here, God already ordered and established your steps. Our jobs is to seek His timing so we can be RIGHT ON TIME with God's plan for our life. The same way your life has ordered steps; your church has ordered steps. Is your church ahead or behind the timing of God?

All of these times help to give us an understanding of time. Misunderstanding timing can be the Achilles heel for many ministries seeking to have major impact in their community. There are other time zones, such as spirit time, time locks, and quantum time, but we will leave those for another time to discuss. Introducing time as an important part of the process will allow your team to adjust for the long haul. We are not trying to become an overnight success; we understand that planting is a commitment of time. Making sure your team is time conscious also allows your core to develop rhythm.

DEVELOPING RHYTHM

Rhythm cannot be underestimated within the context of building. If you have ever had to do something hard for an extended period of time, you understand the value of rhythm. Within the weightlifting world, in order to build muscles you have to do reps, which is short for repetition. A repetitive exercise focuses the attention on developing a particular area of the body. When it comes to building a church, planting a house or starting a movement, rhythm must be set and adhered to.

I am a very pioneering person. I am not satisfied for very long, and can sometimes skip over achievements and victories for the purpose of reaching further. This can be very dangerous, not to mention discouraging. I had to learn that sometimes being consistent is the greatest victory when it comes to planting. Consistency is key to building any entity that is significant. The ability to delay gratification, being totally focused, and not quitting until the job is done is a skill only developed by disciplined rhythm. What is rhythm? Rhythm is defined as a strong, regular, repeated pattern of movement or sound. Predictability is one of the best ways to develop trust. Many visitors and volunteers love our ministries, but cannot trust them because we don't have rhythm. Now, in no way am I saying that we should become rigid or religious, but I am simply saying that it is hard for people to become great at something, if the rules are always changing. One Sunday we do it this way, and the next Sunday we have changed the format entirely. This type of unpredictability causes people and leaders to begin to doubt our stability.

In the early stages of development, people must be able to count on the stability and consistency of your leadership, your teaching and your service. This part of ministry development can be boring, but the sooner you implant this within the dynamics of your house, the better. This stage of planting is marked by the continual sound of hammers hitting nails. Can you imagine if you were Noah, building the ark? Day in, and day out, not only are you committed to building the ark, but preaching the same message. It's this place where commitment is tested and humility is forged. Can you do the same thing, over and over, without any visible sign of growth or impact? Many leaders start a work, just to find something more "exciting" to do, because planting took too long. Planting takes time, but can cause much fatigue if you do not develop rhythm.

> *6 I have planted, Apollos watered; but God gave the increase. 7 So then neither is he that planteth any thing, neither he that watereth; but God that giveth the increase. 8 Now he that planteth and he that watereth are one: and every man shall receive his own reward according to his own labour. 9 For we are labourers together with God: ye are God's husbandry, ye are God's building. (1 Cor. 3:6-9)*

We are not called to labor alone. Paul, speaking to the church at Corinth, admits that help is needed. While Paul planted, Apollos watered, but God inevitably did the increasing. You cannot deal with the issue of planting without addressing waterers. Every ministry needs waterers. Waterers can be voices from outside of your ministry that release a consistent and respected stream of teaching and support into your house, or waterers can be the leadership core of the church. In both cases, there must be stress put on rhythm. The waiting period is a great time to develop rhythm. It is in between the sowing and the reaping that you work on transforming your leadership from a group to a team. Learning how to work together does not just happen, it must be intentional. Learning how to successfully utilize the chemistry of your team happens during the waiting period. It is in the waiting room of ministry that God works out the kinks and smoothes out the rough spots. The waiting room can be the most tedious time because you do not know when you are going to be called, but be encouraged, your name is on the list.

When we speak about developing rhythm, we are talking about discovering the stride that works best for you, your team, and the house you are building. This involves everything from how often you meet, who does the work, and even the frequency of fellowships. This developing of rhythm is seen with David. David was one of the most prolific worshipers in the Bible. David is said to be a man after God's own heart, which literally means David was syncopated with the heart of God. The heart beats in rhythm, and I believe what gave David the power he had, is that he understood the rhythm of God. Worshipers must understand the rhythm of God. Everything that God does, He does in rhythm. God is beginning and end, He is first and last, He is Alpha and Omega, He is eternal, like a circle, our God works in rhythm. We see this very clearly in the first chapter of Genesis. The Bible says "the evening and the morning" was the first, second and third day, and so forth. God works in rhythm, or revolutions, we call them cycles or seasons. I believe David understood something about this.

In 2 Samuel, chapter 6, we get a very intimate look at the worship life of David. After Saul has ruled over a nation that hasn't seen the glory of God in years, David decides to go and get the Ark of the Covenant. The Ark of the Covenant represents the very presence of the Lord. Can you imagine planting a church that grows without glory? Can you fathom leading a church that has never seen the power of God? David said, "I've got to have the glory." After Israel gets the Ark back, they put it on a new cart, it stumbles and shakes when it passes Nachon's threshing floor, Uzzah reaches out to grab it and is killed by God because of his lack of reverence. David tried to use a Philistine technique to carry something that only Israel was designed to carry. This is a lesson of vision and protocol. The waiting room will always reveal those who are called to carry the vision, and those who are not. The waiting room is the place of development and discovery, but also a place of vulnerability and testing. It is in the waiting room where people will come and make you second guess the word of God over your life and ministry. People will beg you to put your vision on a new cart. It is in the waiting room where people will offer seemingly great ideas, but remember when turbulent times come, the only thing that will remain is what God spoke. We have to be careful not to allow what is popular to distract us from purpose.

David sees the effects of mishandling the vision, or the Ark of God. So in an effort to regroup, he puts the Ark into Obededom's House. Now something strange happens when the Ark of God rests there. The Bible says for three months, everything that pertained to Obededom was blessed. See, what did not work for David, worked for another house. Just because it is working for the church down the street, does not mean it is going to work for you. The plan and purpose of God for your church must be so important, that you are willing to look unsuccessful for a season, so that the blessing of God could rest in your house. All that David did to get the Ark back, and now he has to let someone else borrow the glory. Here is another word for you, just because someone else is being successful, doesn't mean you are not. When God blesses someone else, many times He is teaching us the correct protocol to being blessed. Now when David finally gets the Ark back, he does something strange.

> 12 And it was told king David, saying, The LORD hath blessed the house of Obededom, and all that pertaineth unto him, because of the ark of God. So David went and brought up the ark of God from the house of Obededom into the city of David with gladness. 13 And it was so, that when they that bare the ark of the LORD had gone six paces, he sacrificed oxen and fatlings. 14 And David danced

before the LORD with all his might; and David was girded with a linen ephod. 15 So David and all the house of Israel brought up the ark of the LORD with shouting, and with the sound of the trumpet. (2 Sam. 6:12-15)

Do you see that? Look at verse thirteen. The Bible says that David took six paces and then stopped to sacrifice oxen and fatlings. Do you see the rhythm of worship? Six is the number of man, and every time David took that sixth step, he stopped and recognized the need for the presence of God and offered a sacrifice. The waiting room is a place of contemplation and meditation. The waiting room is the place you come face to face with your limitation. It is in the waiting room that you get time to think and ponder about how great God is. You are not distracted by the hustle and bustle of ministry, you have freedom to relax and praise God. We can get very busy planting, and soon forget that we need God. A growing church, a family, marketing, and leadership can eclipse God, but the waiting room is the remedy. It doesn't matter how fast you are going, there are times that God has to slow you down and remind you who He really is. Do you mind waiting?

The Forgotten Ingredient: Morale

Planting a church takes a lot of focus. Most church planters are workaholics. We work long hours, fighting to be free from distractions that most time we miss our true calling. Planting is about people. So many times we are so determined to grow, that we forget about the people who are plowing with us. I have seen more ministries fail because of bad morale, than from a lack of people or resources. Morale, I believe, is the forgotten ingredient within leadership. It is the missing link between good and great organizations. What is morale? Morale is defined as the confidence, enthusiasm, and discipline of a person or group at a particular time. A team or ministry only works at the level of their morale. Waiting can really wear down the morale of a team.

And let us not be weary in well doing: for in due season we

159

shall reap, if we faint not. (Galatians 6:9)

The word "weary" there means utterly exhausted or spiritless. If your team or ministry seems to be dragging, it may be a morale issue. Morale is a delicate subject, and even more sensitive to deal with. Morale is known to be a critical ingredient to success, and when morale isn't present failure is sure to come. To lead unenthusiastic people can suck the life out of you, and drain you of energy. Many pastors dread coming to church because of passionless people. There are a few things that lead to low morale:

1. Lack of Vision
2. Lack of Leadership
3. Lack of Communication
4. Lack of Encouragement
5. Heavy Workloads
6. Lack of Relationships
7. Losing Focus
8. Lack of Teamwork
9. Lack of Empowerment or Autonomy
10. Fear of Failure
11. Perfectionism
12. Comparison

There are many more that we could add, but this seems to be the common consensus. I cannot deal with each one, but the one I did want to highlight is the fear of failure. Very soon after we launched Embassy International, I told our leadership we were going to live in the "Try Dimension" for a while. Now you are saying, what in the world is the "try dimension"? Fear is a spirit. Fear is a spirit that comes to suffocate faith, and paralyze your purpose. Fear does not want you to move. Fear wants you to focus on the problem, and not on the promise. Fear loves doubt, and is deathly afraid of risk takers. The Bible says that God has not given us the spirit of fear. Well if God did not give it to us, why would we want it? I don't know about you, but I don't want anything that God has not given me. The fear of failure usually is grown within a house whose leader is a perfectionist. I understand this well, because I was victim to this. When you are growing a church, you want it to be perfect. From the parking lot, to the pulpit, to the pew, you want everything in order and ready to amaze. But, the truth is, on your way to excellence there will be many failures. If you want your team to be free and open, you have to give them the right to fail. Notice, I did not say the right to be a failure, but you have to show them that there is a blessing in making mistakes. We want every service perfect, but if we do not allow room for people to grow, our church becomes legalistic. You want people to be free to fail. I told our team, "look, we are going to try a whole bunch of stuff, some will be God, some will be me. If we fail, it's ok, we will just admit that that was me, and not God." As a leader you have to have the capacity to say, "that wasn't God." It is all right for you to be wrong. As a matter of fact, the sooner you break the mindset off of your team that you are perfect, the sooner you will be free to move in the creativity of God. It is in this realm, the creativity of God, where people are productive. If you make people afraid of failure that will never step out of the boat.

COMPARISON KILLS AUTHENTICITY

Waiting can be a frustrating season. It's nothing like being in traffic, anticipating arriving at your destination just to be halted by an endless array of bad drivers. I have found out by riding with many people, that everyone is crazy. Have you every felt that way, like no one can drive but you? I feel that way all the time. Waiting brings out the best in us, but it also reveals the worst in us. There is nothing that challenges our patience like being stuck in traffic. In traffic you get to see a lot. You get to see people who aren't really paying attention, they're texting or talking on the phone. You see people picking their nose or yelling at kids. When you are in traffic you see cars that are on your vision board, and you also see cars you wouldn't be caught dead in.

I've discovered that most ministries suffer from a severe case of road rage. Have you ever been cut off in traffic, just to find yourself yelling, maybe even cursing at someone who can't hear you anyway? These moments of insanity can ruin our day and sometimes alter our moods completely. I know a few people that have extreme road rage problems, and I am sure you know some as well. There have been reported cases of people actually falling victim to road rage, being assaulted and sometimes even killed. We are all rushing to a place that's not moving, and many times we are willing to kill each other to get there. Ministry is very similar. We are willing to kill other churches in our city just to grow and be "successful." The waiting room can be an ugly place. When you are sitting in the waiting room, or stuck in traffic, one of the things that kill ministries is comparison. Comparison in ministry is a dangerous sickness. Like cancer, comparison wants to grow and consume every area of your life until you are too discouraged to continue.

> *For we dare not make ourselves of the number, or compare ourselves with some that commend themselves: but they measuring themselves by themselves, and comparing themselves among themselves, are not wise. (2 Cor. 10:12)*

Paul is clear that it is unwise to compare. We are all called to specific assignments, how can we then dare to compare ourselves with others. I have had people look at my anointing, and then ask me where I got it from. After I told them my story, they actually tried to live the life I lived in order to get what is on my life. The anointing does not transfer by mimicking; it transfers by impartation, and is activated by submission and service. Comparison is rife within ministry. We want to preach like the best preachers, we want to heal like the best healers, all the while killing our uniqueness. Comparison kills authenticity. When you compare yourself with another, what you are saying is "God, I don't really like what you have given me. I want what they have." These statements are usually made subconsciously, but always prematurely. Most people have never walked to the edge of their gift and anointing to even see there true potential.

You are a masterpiece. There has never been, and will never be a gift like you. What you have to learn is how to work what you have. Once you learn the dynamics of your own gift, you will never be jealous of anyone else ever again. Paul also deals with the issue of measuring. He says that they measure themselves by themselves. When you are isolated and only surround yourself with people like you, you miss the benefit of exposure and diversity. When you have only been exposed to a certain people group or denomination, your view can be very limited. Paul actually says that people, who do this, are unwise. You cannot measure the success of your ministry based on someone else's house. You only compare your ministry with the vision that God has given you, and how it measures up to that. So the question you must ask is, "What am I building?" Once you are completely convinced about the blueprint that the Lord has given you, there is no way that comparison can ever distract you again.

Rainbows and Pots of Gold

Chapter Seven

Building Legacy by Raising Sons

There was once a young man, full of potential, who was the son of a wealthy business owner. He hated living under the shadow of his father, always feeling the pressure of his accomplishments. "I want to be my own man," the boy would yell in frustration. Every achievement his father would procure would only enrage the boy even further. After consistent pressure over the years the boy decided to move out. "Dad, I have decided to move out. I am starting my own business as well," the boy said arrogantly. The father, with tears in his eyes, heart broken, thinking about the years of sacrifice and labor spent to give his son a head start in life. The father did not want to see his son struggle like he did, nor did he want his son to have to start from scratch. The son refused to reconsider and ask the father for his portion of the will. The father overcome with grief, feeling betrayed to his core, relinquishes the young man's inheritance. The son left, and the father never heard from him again, until one sunny day. The father, outside working, sees a tiny figure in the distance. The father cannot make out what it is, but there is expectation in his heart. The father starts running. As the father, who is old in age, begins to tire, he finds strength and faith. With no regard for his own life, he runs, gasping for air. "It's him, it's him," the father screams with tears filling his eyes. They collide, causing an explosion like an atomic bomb. The father is overjoyed, throws a party for the young man, and welcomes him home. The young man is restored, healed and reconciled to his father.

In Luke, chapter 15, we get a glimpse of the heart of God in a very intimate way. We are all familiar with the story of the prodigal son, and how he demanded the portion of goods that fell to his and went and spent all he had on riotous living. The boy, lying in the midst of pigs, comes to himself and returns home. This story is about more than a lost son, it is about a lost generation. Sons represented, in these days, the future of a family. When the father lost his son, he was losing so much more than just a family member; he was losing hope for the future. I believe that we are in a very pivotal time in the Body of Christ, which the story of the prodigal son depicts vividly. This parable is actually the story of an age and time that I believe we are in now.

> *God, who at sundry times and in divers manners*
> *spake in time past unto the fathers by the*
> *prophets, 2 Hath in these last days spoken unto us*
> *by his Son... (Hebrews 1:1-2)*

This is the age of sons. When God wants to do anything, He raises a son. Sons are sent to complete assignments. In this chapter I want to deal with the sonship issue. In a time where everyone is asking for the portion of goods that falls to them, we desperately need sons. In a world that awards dishonor, and celebrates disrespect and rebellion, we need sons. No ministry can survive without sons. If you hope to build anything significant, you will need sons. Sons work without wage, always seeking their father's heart. It is a dangerous position to be sonless. So in this chapter we will to speak to the importance of fathers and their function, the purpose and powers of sons, and the mechanism of mantles. This portion of our journey is designed to restructure your garden into a home. The first organization that God sanctioned was the family, and it is this that becomes the power model for our churches. Most churches model themselves after businesses, and while they flourish financially, they lack power and sincerity. The only way to grow a church that will truly carry the heart of Jesus is by understanding the need for fathers and sons.

THE TECHNOLOGY OF GENERATIONS

When Adam was created, he was an eternal being. Adam, being made in the image and likeness of God, had no expiration date. Can you imagine having an unlimited amount of time to complete your assignment? Most leaders don't feel as if they have enough time to do what God has called them to do. Well, this was not the world that Adam was acquainted with. God gave Adam limitless ability. Adam was not bound by time or age. But then, Adam fell. When Adam fell he became limited by time. How do we know this?

> But of the tree of the knowledge of good and evil, thou shalt not eat of it: for in the day that thou eatest thereof thou shalt surely die. (Gen. 2:17)

Death only makes sense within the context of time. We understand that death is separation, but it is also the cessation of life. Death begins when life ends. As soon as the fruit from the Tree of the Knowledge of Good and Evil touched his lips, Adam began to age. Once this occurs, God initiates what I call the technology of generations.

Adam knew his wife Eve, and they bore sons. Sons became Adam's tool of continuation. Adam was now limited to a certain time called a life span. It was within this life span that Adam needed to complete his assignment, or his purpose would be aborted, and the plan of God would cease in the earth. Adam needed a way around this, and that way was sons. The technology of generations is the tool that God uses to extend time so that assignments never spoil before their completion. As a father would diligently work within his generation, a son would be born to continue his work. A son has to, of his own will, lay down his life to and intentionally live the life of his father. In a generation that is screaming, "I want to be my own man," there must arise sons who die selflessly to fulfill their father's assignment. We have killed the understanding and importance of sons by teaching personal purpose to an extreme, but you can ask Jesus, the Son of God had no purpose outside of His father. Fathers impart purpose. When Cain and Abel were born, Adam and Eve shouted for joy, there was now someone to continue the family business of being fruitful, multiplying, replenishing, subduing and expanding God's dominion. The devil gets a whiff of this new technology that has entered the Earth and uses Cain to try and stop the plan of God, but it's too late, humanity can now have babies. The kingdom of darkness is afraid whenever a church gets pregnant. Whenever a city, a nation, or a house gets pregnant, all of hell begins to tremble. Seth is raised up, so is Enoch and Noah, Abraham and Joseph, and one by one they take up the baton to continue this assignment. We even see this with Jesus. Jesus did not come without picking up the baton. Jesus comes to John at the river Jordan and says, "baptize me," or in other words, "pass the baton." The disciples pick it up, and the only reason you are reading this book is because even you have decided to pick up the baton. The technology of generations is needed if we are going to see city transformation. The revival we want to see must be built, but it is going to take the power of generations. The transformation that we are looking to experience will be multigenerational; it cannot stop with you. How do we see this transformation take place? Sons!

Whenever there is not a father in position, a generation has to start over. Starting from scratch is an extremely difficult thing to do. When a generation has to start over, without the wisdom, endorsement or experience of the past, we lose time. Now remember, because of Adam's fall, time is a very precious commodity. Everything is measured in time. Your age, your wage, the day, everything is measured in time. Time is one of the most precious commodities that you have, and it is extremely expensive. Time is like money, it is finite, and once you spend it, it's gone. The same way we budget money, we must budget out time. Realize that, just like money, if you spend time in one place, you eliminate your ability to use that time in another place. Budget your time wisely. Who you spend time with, what you spend time entertaining, and where you spend your time are of utmost importance. Time is finite, and we cannot afford to start over. Everyone in our day wants their own thing. Churches are dwindling down because everyone wants to be a pastor now. No one wants to serve; everyone wants to be the center of attention.

Knowing that whatsoever good thing any man doeth, the same shall he receive of the Lord, whether he be bond or free. (Ephesians 6:8)

When we submit and serve the previous generation, God blesses us to be fruitful and successful in our calling. In order for this age of sons to be entered into, we are going to have to change what we preach and how we preach in our house. This is why this chapter is so important for the church planter and leader. The sooner you begin to birth sons, which we will detail later, the sooner your ministry has the stability to move forward. Establishing legacy within a house takes time and sacrifice, but the rewards are great in the kingdom of God.

THE FUNCTION OF FATHERS

The understanding of spiritual fathers is still a hard truth for the Body of Christ to swallow. This is not a doctrinal issue, this is an honor issue. Before we get into the function of fathers and their purpose, we have to deal with the dynamics of honor. We live in a culture of dishonor. In our chapter, *Greenhouses and Habitats*, we listed the different cultures that should be established in a house, honor should be on the top of the list. I did not add it, because sadly it was not something that I saw consistently demonstrated in churches that were successful. The frightening truth is that we have learned how to do ministry without honor. Everywhere you look, we see dishonor. Children speak against their parents, while parents discourage and curse their children. We speak against leadership, dignitaries, and authorities, and then ponder why our children vehemently disrespect us. Dishonor runs rampant in our generation.

What is honor? Honor is the recognition and right response to rank. Every Kingdom is structured according to rank. Rank refers to the relative position, value, worth, complexity, power, importance, authority, level etc. of a person or object. Ranks are levels of gifting, anointing and authority. While we are all equally loved by God, we are not all equally anointed by God. Honor recognizes an individual's rank and responds to it. For example, when we were young, we were taught that young children don't talk while an adult is talking. Why? Because their conversation outranked ours. I have seen young ministers and preachers sit down with living legends and try to offer advice. This is dishonor. When you are in the presence of great men, the best thing you can do is shut up, and learn something. Because America is a democracy, we have raised a democratic church. We vote on everything, we do comment cards and we always want to know what the congregation thinks about the decisions we are making. My question is, what does God think about your decisions? Don't put the destiny of your church into the hands of man's opinions. Because we are a democratic culture, we have been taught that everyone's opinion matters. We allow everyone to have a voice, freedom of speech, even if they are not talking about anything relevant. Democracy diminishes rank, and breeds a generation of dishonor. The Kingdom of God is not a democracy, it is a kingdom. Every kingdom is structured by rank and order. Family has rank and order. The highest rank within a family is the father, next is the mother, and last is the son. The father's presence within the home is not an option, it is a necessity. This is not just true of a family, but also true of an apostolic house or kingdom center. Every church needs a father. What makes a house? It is the Spirit of a Father. Not just the Spirit of Father God, but also the Spirit of Fatherhood. When there is the Spirit of a Father in a house, it makes that house a HOME. A Father provides vision, strategy, protection and direction. Without the Father, generational production is not possible. Being a pastor will no longer suffice. We have a generation of Joshuas that are looking for their Moses.

The office of the pastor and the office of an apostle, or apostolic father, are very different. Now these differences need to be understood if we are going to move our churches from the sheep level into the son level. Most churches are filled with sheep. Sheep lack intelligence and vision, they produce meat, wool and milk, but cannot carry legacy. Sons are mature gifts submitted to the vision of the house and the heart of the father. The anointing of the pastor is to nurture, while the anointing of the apostle is to build. The anointing of the pastor is to guard, while the apostle governs. The pastor focuses on organization, while the father focuses on order. I believe that without the presence of a father, a church can not reach it's full potential. It takes a father to raise a son. It takes a father to awaken destiny inside of a house.

> *3 Now Israel loved Joseph more than all his children, because he was the son of his old age: and he made him a coat of many colours. 4 And when his brethren saw that their father loved him more than all his brethren, they hated him, and could not speak peaceably unto him. 5 And Joseph dreamed a dream, and he told it his brethren: and they hated him yet the more. (Gen. 37:3-5)*

I want you to notice that Joseph never dreamed until his father covered him with a coat. This is not the only time we see this.
We also see this throughout the Bible, especially in the book of Acts.

> *16 But this is that which was spoken by the prophet Joel; 17 And it shall come to pass in the last days, saith God, I will pour out of my Spirit upon all flesh: and your sons and your daughters shall prophesy, and your young men shall see visions, and your old men shall dream dreams: 18 And on my servants and on my handmaidens I will pour out in those days of my Spirit; and they shall prophesy. (Acts 2:16-18)*

Notice it was only until the Father covered them with the Holy Spirit that they began to have vision and dreams. This is a principle. We see this in the life of Jesus, for Jesus did no miracles until the Father covered him at His baptism. Father God gave Jesus a coat of many colors. Fathers ignite a passion in their sons for the purposes of God. Fathers call sons into their rightful position as heirs in the Kingdom of God. Without the father present, congregants have to push and force their way into purpose, many times lacking the advantage of definition. Fathers define. Fathers define roles, responsibilities, and rights. A church that is solely administrated by a pastor will be ran by the heart, while apostolic churches tend to be very heady. This is why I believe that every house needs the presence of all five grace gifts (apostle, prophet, evangelist, pastor and teacher) in order to have kingdom balance.

The pastoral model of ministry has been very important as it relates to bringing us out of the bondage of traditionalism into the power of the promise. The heart of God for this hour is that we see the reinstitution of fathers within the house of God. A father within a house is not satisfied with servants and slaves; fathers need sons. Fathers put pressure on the house to produce and not just engage in programs. The father's job is to establish vision and direction for the house. All through out the Bible we see apostolic models of fathers. I think one of the great models of a father is Moses. Moses was a dynamic father.

And Joshua the son of Nun was full of the spirit of wisdom; for Moses had laid his hands upon him: and the children of Israel hearkened unto him, and did as the LORD commanded Moses. (Deut. 34:9)

Joshua, as a son, was submitted under the hand of Moses. What does this mean? Joshua allowed Moses to shape and mold him into the image of Christ. Like clay in the hand of the potter, the son was in the hand of his father, being molded into his purpose. There is a blessing in the father's hands. God puts resources in the hands of those who have been given stewardship over us, but sons must allow the shaping. Most sons already have in their minds, who they want to be, so when the father begins to shape them, they rebel. The son must give up his right of identity to be fashioned into the image of the father. Please understand that I am speaking dimensionally. This is true of our heavenly Father, our spiritual fathers and our natural fathers. What makes us reject fathers? Honor. Honor is a source of power.

Honour thy father and thy mother: that thy days may be long upon the land which the LORD thy God giveth thee. (Exodus 20:12)

Children, obey your parents in the Lord: for this is right. 2 Honour thy father and mother; (which is the first commandment with promise;) 3 That it may be well with thee, and thou mayest live long on the earth. (Eph. 6:1-3)

Notice that Paul says that this commandment is the first one with promise. Honor brings a reward. The Kingdom of God is a reward system, and the highest seed you can sow is the seed of honor. Let's look at the rewards of honor. Honor brings long life. If honor brings long life, dishonor cuts your life short. I believe it is dishonor that has allowed for an abundance of untimely deaths among our youth. Not only does honor produce longevity, but honor makes sure things are well with you. This is the place of favor. Honor brings favor, dishonor brings famine. Honor is the key to the manifestation of promises in our life. Honor is a culture that we must grow in our houses, in our families and communities.

The Bible says that Joshua was "filled" with wisdom, because Moses laid his hands on him. Moses unleashed a massive degree of impartation in the life of Joshua because Joshua honored Moses. Honor opened up a channel of blessing and impartation in the life of Joshua. When honor is absent, there cannot be true impartation. What does honor look like? A house that builds a culture of honor has a distinct look and feel. A house of honor celebrates diversity, encouraging everyone to be who God has called them to be. Honor creates an environment where everyone feels valuable and needed. Church planter, when you do not value a gift, that gift will soon leave. We must honor our leaders, those over and under us, and we must honor the sacrifice of the congregation. Building a culture of honor happens by intentionally showing gratitude and highlighting the service of those who labor with us. Here are some ways honor should be built:

1. Always acknowledge the sacrifice and dedication of those who make the service happen. This includes, but is not limited to, the senior leadership, the core leadership and volunteers.
2. Always create an opportunity for others to serve and get

involved. Establishing a ministry where everyone serves is rare, but is needed for those houses that intend to have longevity.

3. Create numerous ways and avenues for people to give. Giving is a part of honor. You cannot separate giving from honor. If someone honors the ministry and/or minister, they will give. Also, I suggest, openly discussing financial goals and objectives, and thanking those who give over and above the call of duty.

4. At Embassy International, we periodically give awards, and deem hard workers as "member of the month." This helps everyone strive for excellence.

These are just a few ways to really cultivate a culture of honor within a house. As you seek the Lord, the Lord will give you creative ways to show and build honor in the church or business you are planting. We need like never before houses of honor and rank. We need kingdom centers that celebrate leadership and take care of those who sacrifice so much to empower people and transform the areas they are planted in. When the senior leadership sows honor, they can expect a harvest of honor to grow that will feed the entire flock. Before we move on, I really want you to grasp how important honor is to the life of your house and the potency of your anointing. Every Joshua needs a Moses. Maybe you are reading this, and you don't have a Moses in your life. Let me tell you this, find your Moses no matter what it costs.

TASTE THE RAINBOW

And I will establish my covenant with you; neither shall all flesh be cut off any more by the waters of a flood; neither shall there any more be a flood to destroy the earth. 12 And God said, This is the token of the covenant which I make between me and you and every living creature that is with you, for perpetual generations: 13 I do set my bow in the cloud, and it shall be for a token of a covenant between me and the earth. 14 And it shall come to pass, when I bring a cloud over the earth, that the bow shall be seen in the cloud: 15 And I will remember my covenant, which is between me and you and every living creature of all flesh; and the waters shall no more become a flood to destroy all flesh. 16 And the bow shall be in the cloud; and I will look upon it, that I may remember the everlasting covenant between God and every living creature of all flesh that is upon the earth. 17 And God said unto Noah, This is the token of the covenant, which I have established between me and all flesh that is upon the earth. (Gen. 9:11-17)

After the flood of Noah, God made a promise that He would never again destroy the Earth with water. God entered into covenant with Noah, and the sign of that covenant was a rainbow. God used this natural phenomenon to remind His people that they were always covered. I believe it is interesting to note that rainbows cannot appear unless there has been rain. It is just like God to remind us of his goodness during rainy seasons of our life. Understand church planter, the rain is needed. On your planting journey there will be much rain, but the rain is meant to grow you. I do not want this book to be a "how to grow your church" book, but rather, I want this book to be a "how to grow you" book. God placed a reminder in the sky of His covenant to His people.

God is a God of covenant. Covenant binds God to His word, and to His people. Without covenant, relationships are void of significance, and never maturing into kingdom connections. Covenant is so important, God entered into covenant with Himself.

For when God made promise to Abraham, because he could swear by no greater, he sware by himself. (Hebrew 6:13)

God is so serious about covenant, that when God made a promise to Abraham, He swore by himself that He would make the promise good. God does not speak a word without taking the necessary steps to fulfill that word. This is why we must be encouraged. If God said build it, if God said plant it, if God said raise it, all of Heaven is backing us to see that word come to pass. Not only does God enter into covenant with Himself, but we enter into covenant with God also. When people accept Christ as their Lord and Savior, what they are doing is entering into covenant. A covenant is binding, and obligates each party to certain duties and responsibilities. All throughout the Bible we see the power of covenant. The revelation of covenant must enter back into our faith. Faith without covenant is like hoping in an empty promise. Our entire faith is based on a promise. Jesus promised us that He would be killed, but He would not stay dead. Jesus promised that He would be raised from the dead, and He was. Covenant is so powerful, it can raise the dead. Covenant is a power source that the Body of Christ has disrespected through dishonor. Nowadays our word means nothing. We tell people we will be there for them, never expecting to be there. We promise our leaders we will cover them, and at the first sign of trouble we leave. We promise our cities we will fight for them, but we move to other regions when we don't see the numerical growth in our churches we desire to see. We need men and women of covenant. One of the greatest examples of covenant in the scripture is the story of Elijah and Elisha.

In first Kings, chapter seventeen, a gift names Elijah comes on the scene out of nowhere. We don't know where he came from, and we don't know where he is going, but he finds a boy named Elisha and history takes a dramatic turn. There are three ways a season changes in a person's life: revelation, opportunity, and connection. Revelation usually comes with a word from God. God can use a person, place or thing to reveal to you the purpose of your location. Every time God speaks a word, seasons change.

The second way seasons change is by opportunity. Whenever you are given an opportunity, there is the possibility, if you handle that moment correctly, that your season will change. When David was called into the courts of Saul to play, that was an opportunity that was going to change his season. When Pharaoh called Joseph on his platform to interpret his dream, which was an opportunity that changed his season. Seasons change as we seize and successfully steward opportunities.

The third way our seasons change is by connections. Every relationship either adds to us, or subtracts from us. Relationships are the currency of the Kingdom. Nothing happens in the Kingdom of God without relationships. Relationships are keys to access new seasons, or old seasons. Have you ever ran into someone you haven't seen in a long time, and they automatically remind you of a place in your past you never want to go back to? But in the same manner, sometimes we meet people who are pictures of our future, and they remind us of the call of God on our life. Elijah was this for Elisha, a reminder of the greatness on his life. Spiritual fathers are this to us. When God sets a man or woman in your life to father you, they become that prophetic picture to remind you of the call of God on your life. Spiritual fathers are not just mentors and coaches; they are divine architects, anointed by God to build you into a vessel of honor and power. The relationship between father and son cannot be made without covenant. Dishonor produces covenant-less houses, and a house that does not understand covenant will never have anything but artificial relationships. I implore you to study, teach, and demonstrate covenant in your church in a radical way.

We must be covenant people. When we are people of covenant, we are people of roots, not tossed to and fro by the cares of life. In order for the Kingdom of God to advance with power, the value of relationships must shift drastically. When planting a church, many times the value is put on vision, programs, and even location. All of these things are important and have their place, but if we are going to see revival built in our cities, it will take covenant relationships. The infancy of our ministry development must be focused on covenant. Without covenant, relationships have no impartational value. Without covenant, relationships are dwindled down into mere associations without the potential to push us forward. We need covenant. Most churches have a revolving door. Many churches see turn over within membership every six months to a year. We cannot develop the lives of people with a six month commitment. Covenant relationships are the root of our houses, and without them we cannot produce fruit. Let us look at a statement of covenant.

And Elijah said unto Elisha, Tarry here, I pray thee; for the LORD hath sent me to Bethel. And Elisha said unto him, As the LORD liveth, and as thy soul liveth, I will not leave thee. So they went down to Bethel. (2 Kings 2:2)

Elijah is about to be taken by a whirlwind, and challenges Elisha to stay behind, but Elisha has a promise. Elijah promised Elisha that if he remained, and saw Elijah when he was taken, Elisha would receive a double portion. This double portion was the birthright, or due inheritance for a son. But notice carefully what the son's job was, to stay put. In a culture that is always changing and accommodating our dysfunction, there must be a generation that says, "I will serve regardless of the season or time." We desperately need a covenant revolution, that says what Elisha said "As the Lord liveth, and as thy soul liveth, I will not leave thee." Do you know what we could accomplish with a stable and secure generation? Do you understand what could be achieved with a planted people? Houses are not hotels where travelers and tourists come to get relaxation, they're homes designed to grow futures. We must challenge our people, and the cultures of our cities and ministries to develop covenant people. I have found that many in the church believe that they are not growing, and most times they blame it on a lack of teaching or opportunity. Understand this, you can only grow according to how deep you have been planted. How far are you willing to go? If you stop, turn back, and quit every time the journey gets rough, you will never grow. But, if you like Elisha declare with covenantal force that you are going nowhere, you can grow to heights unimaginable.

Every son needs a father, and every father needs a son. Without covenant, this relationship cannot be forged. Covenant is the foundation for power relationships. Covenant is the cement that binds us together regardless of season, distance, or problem. Make a covenant with your people, and challenge them to make a covenant with you, that we will build something significant in this city that will transform generations not yet born. Planting a church is inspirational at its core. For a person to look at a barren field and hope is a heartfelt thing. For a person to look at a broken life, and say, "they can live again," is an empowering thing. Church planter, you are called to do more than plant a church, you are called to empower a city, to bring hope to a generation, to inspire a people, and to transform a nation. Do not look at your job as small, for it is all but that.

THE PURPOSE OF SONS

Building generational churches takes time and work. Building a church that is generational takes more than finances and popularity, it takes sons. Sons are the hope of a future. Sons are the destiny of nations. Now let us deal with the theology of sons. When we talk about sons, we are not dealing with gender, but rank. In every house there are two classes, those who are set by authority, and those who are set by assignment. The authority class is usually made up of the father and mother, while the assignment class is made up of sons. The reason this distinction is important is because we must understand that the highest rank assignment in a house is sonship. We must kill the notion that the highest position is behind the pulpit. The greatest thing you can hold as a son, is not a microphone, but the heart of your father.

> For unto us a child is born, unto us a son is given: and the government shall be upon his shoulder: and his name shall be called Wonderful, Counsellor, The mighty God, The everlasting Father, The Prince of Peace. 7Of the increase of his government and peace there shall be no end, upon the throne of David, and upon his kingdom, to order it, and to establish it with judgment and with justice from henceforth even for ever. The zeal of the LORD of hosts will perform this. (Isa. 9:6-7)

Notice that as Isaiah prophesies the coming of the Messiah he uses two different words to describe his purpose and progression. Isaiah says that children are born, but sons are given. There is a difference between children and sons. Paul deals with the juvenile dimension in the epistle he writes to the Corinthian church.

> *When I was a child, I spake as a child, I*
> *understood as a child, I thought as a child: but*
> *when I became a man, I put away childish things.*
> *(1 Cor. 13:11)*

Paul says when I was a child, signifying that this is a stage of development. This word "child" is the Greek word *nepios*, which literally means one that does not have the capacity to speak. This word also means an infant, a juvenile, an immature Believer, or a simple-minded person. Children are only concerned with themselves. Children are selfish, instinctive, and unreliable. When a church is filled with children, that house will be unstable. Children cannot reproduce, and if you ask any parent, sometimes children discourage you from reproducing. Children can be a headache to deal with, but they bring joy. I don't think there is anything more rewarding than to see someone newly born again, and/or accepting Jesus as their Lord and Savior for the first time. But we must be careful not to become so overjoyed by a new birth that we forget that at some point this child has to grow up. Have you ever met a parent that dreads the maturity of their child, believing that when their child grows up they will forget about the parent? Some pastors and parents struggle with this issue of maturing children because of a fear that they might someday leave. Pastors intentionally put entire congregations on milk diets, never transitioning them to meat, because they are afraid of being abandoned and alone. As fathers we must understand our responsibility and obligation to grow mature men and women for the furtherance of the Kingdom of God.

A generational church is one who transcends their current generation. When we mention a generational church, we are not just dealing with the age of the partners, but the ability to transition the church past the life span of the current set man or woman. The best way for a church to plan for generations is to raise up sons. Remember, sonship is not determined by gender, but by maturity. Isaiah says that sons are given. I love this statement. The Bible says, "For God so loved the world, that He gave His only begotten Son," sons are given. Sons are gifts that are given to a generation. Why are sons a gift? Because they provide a future. Without a son, the future will be disappointed. Sons are given for assignments. Sons are assignment focused. Joshua had an assignment in the life of Moses, so did Elisha in the life of Elijah, and so did Timothy in the life of Paul. Sons are driven by the assignment to please their fathers. When we look at the life of Jesus, He was on an assignment. From an early age He understood His assignment. Do you remember when Mary and Joseph lost Jesus in the temple as a young boy? Mary, having a maternal meltdown, says, "Where were you," and Jesus responds with ancient wisdom, "I must be about my Father's business." This is a profound revelation of sonship. Sons are about their father's business, not their own. Generational plans are aborted when sons don't steward the business of their fathers well. A son must be consumed with his father's business. True sons are born to serve.

The word "son" in the Greek is *huios*, and it connotes a full grown or mature individual. A son is one who has grabbed the heart of his father, and has proven himself worthy of rank and responsibility to handle his father's business. The story of the prodigal son gives us a great picture of the transformation and development of a son. When the prodigal son goes to his father and asks for his inheritance, this is the child level. Children have no respect for protocol, order or timing. Children yell when they are hungry, cry when they are frustrated, and throw tantrums when they do not get their way. Does this sound like anyone in your business, family, or congregation? When a church is filled with children, ask Moses, all you will hear is nonstop whining. The prodigal son asks for the portion of goods that fell to him, and then goes and spend it on riotous living, or purposeless activities. Children don't know what to do with inheritances. Children will waste a gift, an anointing, a platform and an opportunity. Children cannot discern seasons, nor can they steward moments.

The prodigal son lacked wisdom, honor, and strategy. The child runs out of money, and finds himself in a pigsty. Jesus said something interesting at one point; He said, "don't cast your pearls to swine." Every son is a pearl. A pearl is shaped by pressure. Pearls are hidden for a season, but when they are revealed they are very valuable. True sons understand the power of being hidden. True sons understand the secret to not being seen. True sons understand the power in obscurity. Church planter, leader, business owner, husband, father, pastor, listen to me, you may be hidden now, but God is developing you into a son. I don't believe the father threw his son into the pigsty; it was the son's immaturity. Pastor, there will always be people who leave you prematurely, this is not in anyway a reflection on you as a father, but it reveals their immaturity as a son. There are people we love, people we care about, people we give our hearts to that will leave us, and the sad truth is that we have to let them go. Holding on to someone that does not want to be held is impossible. But the pressure of the pigsty produced a pearl. All of a sudden this child became a son, and gets up and returns to his father. Sons are able to take responsibility for their actions, while children always play the blame game. Adam was a son, but once he sinned, he was demoted to a child. When God came looking for Adam, and asked Adam why did he eat the fruit, Adam played the blame game. Sons own up to their mistakes and failures and accredit all of their successes to their fathers. Sons are selfless, abhorring attention or accolades. Sons understand I can only go as high as my father, so they make their life's mission to push their father as high as they can.

If we are going to grow powerful ministries, we need sons. We do not need bastards, we do not need fans, we don't need groupies, we need sons. We need men and women with the ability to reproduce after our hearts. When we focus on growing sons, our ministries will take on a different focus and culture. Ministries that major in the development of sons become launching pads for the next generation of leaders and world changers. Don't focus on growing a church, focus on growing sons, and in order to do that, you have to plant yourself. Plant yourself in the lives of those committed to you. Plant yourself in the life of your city and generation, and you will see a harvest that will confuse the world.

DEALING WITH DEPRESSION

I want to get very personal for just a moment. As I am writing this, I am on an airplane, flying back to my city from preaching at a covenant brother's church of mine. We had a powerful time. We saw miracles and healing, it was truly a supernatural time. I preached two messages over the course of two days. One message was "The Breaking Power of the Blessing" and the other was, "Money Miracles." I witnessed things I'd never seen before that week. On our way to the airport, my covenant brother, and me had a very touching conversation. He revealed to me that he is often depressed, and without hesitation I was able to share with him my battles with depression as well. This was not the first time a pastor told me they struggled with depression, and I can promise you that it won't be my last. Maybe you are reading this saying "I struggle with depression too," or maybe you know someone who struggles with depression. I want to end this book, not dealing with branding or marketing, the purpose of multisite campuses, or how to grow your church, but I want to deal with depression.

I know you are wondering why I want to deal with the subject of depression, but for every leader out there, for every pastor who is reading this book, for everyone plowing in the fields of ministry, you understand why. I do not want to deal with depression exhaustively, but I want to touch on it for the sake of encouraging someone. You may not have a name or face that the world knows yet, but you feel the burden of greatness on your life. Knowing that you are destined to do great things is a heavy weight to carry. Heaviness, when it is not alleviated through support and exhortation, can weigh the minister down and make him or her ineffective. Whether you know it or not, many leaders struggle with depression. Everyday leaders are pioneering to produce great things that will change their world, this is an intense assignment. Most pastors, after they finish preaching, they go home and feel so alone. Depression makes you feel alone in a crowded room. Depression makes you feel rejected around loved ones. Depression makes you feel worthless when you are greatly gifted. Have you ever felt depressed?

Depression has been clinically pronounced as a disorder, and it can be. Depression can be hereditary, we accept that. But we cannot be ignorant of the fact that depression is also a spirit. When I say that depression is a spirit, I mean that it is more that physiological, it is spiritual. Most people who struggle with depression cannot always trace it physically; in fact a lot of people cannot find a reason why they are sad. Depressed people are not always unsuccessful people, quite the contrary. Successful people often struggle with depression. I believe successful people struggle with depression because of the nagging question that lingers in the mind of every leader, "am I making a difference?" It is a struggle to lead people who betray you, don't trust you, gossip about you, or don't understand you. It is a struggle giving your life to people that make you constantly wonder, "do they really get it?" Most of you reading this book ask these questions, and honestly I can't tell you they'll ever be answered, but I can tell you that God knows.

One of the ways that you deal with depression is being accountable. Accountability is needed, not just between fathers and sons, but also between leaders. As leaders, brothers and sisters, fellow ministers of the gospel, we have to see the need for lateral accountability like never before. Ministries are being aborted, cities are broken, and destinies disappointed because our leaders are depressed. I want to encourage you church planter, every sleepless night that you have, every tear you shed, every message you preach to heal people while you are broken, Jesus sees it, and your reward is great in the Kingdom of God. I cannot say that planting will be easy, nor can I say that it will yield the fruit that you desire. But, I can promise you that if you are willing to get your knees dirty, and thrust your hands into the soil of your region, God will be proud. I can't promise that you will have the biggest church, but I can promise, if you listen to the voice of the Lord and obey, your city will be impacted and changed. If you follow the rainbow, you will find the pot of gold.

EPILOGUE

This has been a journey. We began discussing the need for a burden in the chapter, *Empty Bellies and Soaked Pillows*. We dealt with the function and purpose of planting within 21st century cities in the chapter, *Floods and Earthquakes*. In that chapter we looked at the dynamics of soil and the agenda of the King to shake cities and communities. In the chapter, *Soldiers and Shoulders*, we looked at the development of teams and the shift from individual ministry to corporate responsibility. We looked at the importance and engineering of vision within the chapter, *Bifocals and Seeing Eye Dogs*, and then discussed culture in the chapter, *Greenhouses and Habitats*. While you are planting, there will be a time of waiting that we all must endure. While we are waiting there are valuable things that we learn and observe. We looked at this briefly in the chapter, *Waiting Rooms and Road Rage*. Lastly, we navigated through the understanding of fathers and sons. We cannot just raise a church of children, but we must produce mature houses filled with sons. It is sons that give our ministries generational power. We scratched the surface of the function of fathers and the purpose for sons in the chapter, *Rainbows and Pots of Gold*.

This book was not designed to be an all-inclusive guide to church planting, but rather a catalyst for a generation of planters to step out, with great faith, and walk on the impossible. My desire is that you plow your city, plant your life and watch God grow something significant. It is not by accident that you read this, nor is it by coincidence that you have decided to invest in your future. You know something great is ahead, you know something ridiculous is just around the corner, you feel something legendary calling. This is my plea, get your knees dirty through prayer and stop at nothing to change your city. My challenge is not that you would start a church, but that you would plant the impossible, so you can see the impossible grow. God bless, change the world.

ACKNOWLEDGMENTS

Before we completely end, I wanted to take a quick moment to mention a few people who have been instrumental in this process. First to my wife and daughter, you guys support me beyond my weaknesses and frailties. To my entire family, I love you guys and without you, I could not have survived this process. To my Executive staff and team, you people are amazing. You continue to keep me accountable, and hold me to a standard of integrity. To the greatest church in the entire world, Embassy International Worship Center, it is a pleasure to pastor and father you. The Lord gave me the greatest honor to be a steward of your development and destiny. To my editing team, and all those that helped make this project a success, you have my heart. A special thank you to CJ Hudgins and Design Cortex. You worked your butt off, and dealt with me even when I was annoying. Thank you to Bishop Bronner. Every since I met you, my life has changed forever. Your wisdom, humility, and insight have revolutionized my life in an incredible way. The moments I spend with you are precious and empower me to complete the assignment over my life. To my covenant partners, friends, and those who continue to pour into my life, Greg Howse, Trent Frank, George Dorton, Benjamin Moore, Antwain Jackson, Jonathan Ferguson, Ricardo Weaver, and Grant Edwards, to all of you I want to say thank you. Special thank you to my sister, Tasha Cobbs, you inspire me more than you know. Our conversations have always made me feel like I can do the impossible. To my brother, Marquis Boone, you are doing a great job man. You are an innovator, and you continue to make me strive for excellence. To everyone that has helped me along the way. I thank you.

Made in the USA
Lexington, KY
26 July 2013